FAITH AND REDEMPTION

FAITH AND REDEMPTION

ELSIE MADRID - MARTINEZ

This book is dedicated to my husband Agustin and my children Angela, Genevieve, Angelo and Marcel.

Agustin, you support me in all that I do and believe in me even when I doubt myself. You are the best husband and Mr. Mom.

Angela, Genevieve, Angelo and Marcel, you are the best kids any parents can have! Each of you add spice and love to my life. It never ends!

Contents

Chapter One

1. Too Early, Too Fast, But Meant to Be

By 1957, President Eisenhower sent Congress a proposal for Civil Rights legislation, and Leonard Berstein's "West Side Story" premiered on Broadway and allowed displays of violence on stage.

My sister was about 6 weeks old when my mother was carrying me. I guess my parents did not wait the 40 days indicated by her physician. Nevertheless, my father's mother was very upset with Mom. "It is too soon for you to have another child. You must abort it as soon as possible!"

My mother, Esther, never had a mother. She passed away when Mami was 18 months old. Mami was raised from home to home. Sometimes, she was with her paternal grandmother, great aunt, or stepmother. There was no stability. She had no idea about how to be a mother or what was the right thing to do. My grandmother did not like Mami because she was not Spanish-looking, and her skin was not fair enough. My father was not supposed to marry her. He had arrived from Colombia to obtain a college education but, instead, went to work to help his family abroad and help his biological mother who lived in New York City. He also liked to party and party hard.

Anyway, my grandmother, Mercedes, recommended that my mother drink quinine to get rid of me. Mami drank quinine and sat in very hot baths. I would not come out! The last resort was to go to the doctor and get a shot to make her period come down—so it was told to me. When this did not work, she returned to her gynecologist a second time to ask for another shot. The doctor said, **"Mire señora, yo no voy a perder mi título. Así que váyase a su casa y tenga su muchachito. Aquí no hay nada más que**

hacer," which means "Look, lady, I am not about to lose my license. Go home and have this child. There is nothing else we can do here." My father did not agree with my mother's decision or his mother's, but their determination was stronger than his to impose their will.

When I was born, both my parents were disappointed because I was not a boy. They said, "Maybe next time."

After just a couple of months, Mom became very worried about me because all I did was move my head back and forth in my playpen or crib. She was totally convinced that I had something going on in my head. She headed to the emergency room, concerned about this situation.

The emergency room was busy, with a long line of patients waiting to be attended. An elderly man who saw me in my mother's arms asked her what she was doing in the emergency room. To his surprise, Mom told him her concern. The man, being advanced in years and wisdom, said,
"Lady, you better take that little girl home. There is nothing wrong with her. Children develop habits when they are growing, and she is an active child. Take her home before the doctors make an experiment out of her, and then, there will really be something wrong with her." My Mom was so scared that she ran out of the emergency room as fast as she had come in.

I am truly a miracle! I truly believe I have a mission in life that the evil one, the prince of the air, knew about, and he needed to destroy me before I was born. I came to know this later in life.

Psalm 139:14, *"I praise you because I am fearfully and wonderfully made; your works are wonderful, I know that full well."*

2. Separation

During the 1960s, there were some strong communities to help people. There were child health stations or clinics located near poor communities. Neighbors looked out for each other. On some occasions, our neighbors, who were on public assistance, shared with other families what their family did not consume. That was how I tasted peanut butter for the first time. Other items shared were butter and American Cheese. I am sure there were other products, but I do not remember.

Papi was a very good provider, but he never turned away a handout. We never went hungry. Mom did not work but used to get asthma often. Dad had to work, come home to wash diapers, clean the dishes, and take care of us. The only thing he would ask Mom was, "Did Mom come to see you today?"

My Mom told me about this later in life. Although my paternal grandmother lived in the same building, I remember my parents being at odds with her. I do not remember her coming to visit us at all. There was no love. Sometimes my sister and I would visit the neighbor because there were children our age. My grandmother would open her door from down the hall to look, and then she would close it without saying a word. As a young child, I found this very strange. How could someone be so cold? Her husband, Juan, was so loving. Sometimes he stopped by to say hello. In this old, dilapidated tenement building, I can still remember that there were two or three apartments on the right of the staircase, and two or three on the left of the staircase.

Grandma did not accept Mom because she was not fair enough. For some reason, some Puerto Rican mothers, who were more Spanish-looking, meaning fair, did not want their sons or daughters marrying someone who was mixed with white and black ancestry. I was told by my Colombian cousin, who happens to be my fourth cousin from my father's side, that my mom and her mother-in-law were friends before Mom married Dad. My grandmother Mercedes was remarried to a kind man named Juan. Apparently, she lived in Cartagena, Colombia, when she first married my father's biological dad. I do not know the entire story about how she came to live in Colombia, but I do know that she lived there for a couple of years before divorcing my grandfather. What I failed to understand is why they divorced in the first place. It has always been a mystery to me why she left her children behind. My father and his sister Mercedes were American-born citizens raised by their father in Cartagena, Colombia, in the town of Canapote. It seems as if every female's name in my family is Mercedes, meaning mercy.

Just to give you a snapshot of the past into this mess, my paternal grandfather remarried a very kind and sweet woman named Catalina. She raised Dad, and his sister, little Mercedes, as her own. Catalina had a younger son, Norton, with my grandfather, but was also raising an older sister named Mercedes. Apparently, my grandfather had a previous relationship with another woman, and the older Mercedes was a daughter from that relationship. Little Mercedes did not last long. Supposedly, she died because no one was paying attention to her when she could not move her bowels. Her stomach hurt, and when taken to the doctor, it was too late. Little Mercedes passed away.

Mom told me that the doctor stated that if little Mercedes could not rid her body of toxins found in her system by vomiting and defecation, she would die. This was my mom's understanding of what happened. Now, Dad was not only separated from his mother, but he was also separated from his younger sister. This separation would later affect his life in ways no one could imagine. His determination in life was to be positive, successful, and he was in so many ways, despite the unfavorable circumstances he found himself in or the problems he created in life from ignorance or self-ambition.

Going back to what happened to Mom, I remember Mom and my sister getting sick one fall morning. Dad had no one to care for us. At the time, my mom had three children. Dad had to take me to this lady named Hilda. I remember my dad bringing in a shopping bag with food. It looked like a food bag.

Hilda was not a nice woman. I was afraid of her apartment because it was gloomy. When I awoke from what I believed was my imagination, screaming, Hilda held out a *chancla,* a slipper, right in front of my face to threaten me. She said, "Shut up, or I'll hit you!" This was said to me with the slipper right in front of my face. Talk about scared, boy was I scared! She had a strange way of worshiping God; I just could not comprehend it. I felt lonely, separated from my parents and siblings. My brother was somewhere else. I guess we were split up because the people who took care of us could only take one of us. I was in this house for a few days while Mom and my sister recuperated at the hospital. My sister, who was eleven months older than me, also had asthma.

Poor Mom did not understand me. Many times, Mom sent me to **Titi's** house, my aunt. I asked too many questions, wet the bed at night, and had too many nightmares. I did not let my parents sleep. **Titi** seemed to understand me. She later became my mentor for life.

One night, I had a bad episode of nightmares, and one of my parents called the ambulance. I remember this woman and a man coming into our apartment with straight jackets. They thought I was a sick kid who was hurting herself or something like that. I remember the lady from the ambulance saying, "Did she hurt herself?" My parents, who did not know any better, said, "She has bad dreams and a vivid imagination and does not let us sleep." These professionals informed my parents that I did not belong in the hospital. I was taken to be evaluated, and Mom said that she had to monitor my television shows. She did not want me to watch any shows that would upset me—like cartoons with violence. I truly believe that being separated from my parents affected me a lot.

I felt left out and was the black sheep of the family. I was not the best behaved at home, and I guess I must have had a lot of tantrums.

I remember my mother telling me that she did not know what to do when I got upset. She was advised by someone to sprinkle some cool water on my face, and this seemed to work.

Separation or changes in my formative years made me very loving and caring because that was what I valued as a child. In my mind, I needed to feel accepted, so I used my God-given talents. I loved people and children. I developed a positive and strong character, no matter what happened.

Isaiah 41:10, *"So do not fear, for I am with you; do not be dismayed, for I am your God. I will strengthen you and help you; I will uphold you with my righteous right hand."*

3. First But Lasting Impressions

During the 1960s, the Hispanic culture was very strict. Children were not supposed to ask adults or parents any questions. You had to do what your parents asked you to do. As a matter of fact, children were to be seen and not heard. God forbid you asked a question and looked at your parents straight in their face. It was considered a lack of respect. They would say, **"Baja la cabeza y no me mires,"** which means "Lower your head, and don't look at me." Can you imagine that? Nowadays, children, for the most part, have no respect for their elders, let alone their parents. Society has gone from one extreme to the other.

It's 1962, and it's time for school, and no one spoke to me about it. I did not know what was happening. All I know is that everyone got dressed to go out. My sister was already attending school. I guess my assumption was to drop her off and return home with Mom.

You see, school, for me, was Romper Room, Bozo the Clown, and other shows. All I knew was that I was in this huge building that looked like a castle from the inside. I do not remember the outside. I guess the inside of this school building left a lasting impression on me.

Since I was attached to my parents, mostly my mother, the thought of attending kindergarten horrified me. I can still remember the majestic vestibule of the school and the banisters leading up the stairs on both sides. I held onto my mother's skirt and refused to meet Mrs. Porter, my kindergarten teacher. When Mom turned her back, I was right behind her. Somehow, I ran away from the teacher, ran down the stairs, and stood behind my mom, who had not left. She was about to leave when I ran down the stairs to catch up with her.

Mom had to take off her *chancla,* slipper, of some sort, to spank my behind. She had to take me back upstairs to the teacher, who was very nurturing, with very blonde hair and blue eyes. Her leg was wrapped in some kind of ace bandage. I have fond memories of her picking me up and saying, "Oh what beautiful earrings you have." I felt such frustration because, although I understood what she was saying, I could not respond in English. How on earth did I learn this language because Mom did not speak a lick of English. Dad spoke English, but he worked nights and slept during the day. Anyway, school life continued, and still, to this day, I remember playing in school and feeling secure after I got over the drama with my mama. The anxiety I felt was terrible, but somehow, my teacher's warm disposition won me over.

Fast forward, I was six years old when President John F. Kennedy was assassinated in Dallas, Texas, in 1963. I recall members of my immediate family watching the wake and funeral of the president on our black and white television set in the living room. Mother was crying inconsolably. I knew the president meant a lot. I could still remember the scene on the screen and the sadness of it all.

Six years old was another milestone. In first grade, I was the line leader on the girl's line because I was the smallest one. During parent-teacher conferences, my teacher told Mami that I always walked too ahead of the class. For some reason, I did everything quickly. My early memories are that I always wanted to be the best.

Learning to read was difficult for me in first grade because Mami did not read or speak English yet. I would say the reading books provided from school were a lot of help. The only book I remember reading was about a boy named Dick, a girl named Jane, and their dog Spot. It was a colorful book. There were no buildings but homes. It was basically a house in the country or the suburbs with a picket fence. I learned to read with this book and wondered about a different way of life. I believe that I lived vicariously through reading. Little did I know that I, too, would be a teacher and would have kindergarten classes for a couple of years before moving up to the higher grades.

"And we know that all things work together for good to those who love God, to those who are called according to His purpose." –**Romans 8:28**

4. Procreation Could Not Be Stopped

The 1960s–1970 was a time when people talked about *population control.* In other words, if families did not control the number of children in their families, the world would literally starve. Families started planning a nuclear family that consisted of two parents and two children. I sometimes heard people talking about one child per parent and not being outnumbered. I think many Hispanics did not believe in this mumble-jumble. Their main concern was to have a reliable job and have enough money to feed their families.

Procreation in my household was inevitable. The forty-day period of recuperation after a baby was born was non-existent. By 1958, Mami had three children in a row, about eleven months apart. However, she got hip to it and found another way of birth control that was effective until a friend suggested another method was better and more secure. Guess what? Baby number four popped out of the clear blue sky. I can still hear Mami saying, "I should have stuck to my method because the minute I changed to the so-called better method, I became pregnant." I remember that belly! It was huge! It was so big Mom felt embarrassed and went out for a walk only after dark with Papi on weekends. It was the late summer season, so it was easier to be out at night.

The doctor recommended that my mother have a cesarean section. It would avoid the bringing down of her organs upon delivery—so Mami told us. It was just like yesterday; I remember one afternoon Mami asked Dad to call the doctor or taxi or something because she had buckets of water gushing out of her birth canal. Not only was the baby big, but he was also about to swim out. There was no pain. My brother Ernest was the most beautiful baby in the nursery. Mami used to say that people visiting the nursery would say, "I want that baby," meaning Ernest, who was 10.5lbs, born to a 5'2 female. His size was so impressive that the nurse was going to hand my baby brother to a large Russian woman who had just delivered. Mami had to show her hospital tags and say, "He's mine."

Although Mami was able to deliver, the doctor had concerns about my mother's postpartum state. He asked my father to allow my mother to get a blood transfusion if Mami was in danger of losing her life; he refused. My mother got wind of this information and took matters into her own hands. She told the doctor, "If I need a transfusion to save my life, I will sign. I am not about to leave my four children as orphans."

My father's faith did not allow any transfusions. According to him, it was against God. Mami was very upset with Dad's decision because he did not consult with her about this serious matter and thought that he had to be out of his mind! As a result, Mami left Dad's denomination and went back to her old ways and returned to the Catholic Church. Mami told me all about this when I was older.

Isaiah 1:18, "'*Come* now, *let us reason together*,' *says the LORD. 'Though your sins are like scarlet, they shall be as white as snow; though they are red as crimson, they shall be like wool.'*"

Chapter Two

1. Winter In the Ghetto

By now, it was about 1964, a time when equal rights were on the scene and on the minds of many Americans. Lydon B. Johnson was president of the United States, who signed the Civil rights Act that would allow people of any color, sex, race, or religion to be treated equally. Furthermore, this meant every citizen would have access to all public places. This act also meant desegregation of schools, and no discrimination was allowed for employment. It also provided equality for African Americans in the Voting Rights Act of 1965. Martin Luther King and many giants of the Civil Rights Movement joined forces with anyone in America who would join them on their marches for equality for all.

Winter was around the corner again, and this meant freezing your butt off in ghetto apartments. For some reason, our apartment was always frigid during the winter months. However, we were not the only ones. Every tenant who lived in one of my landlord's buildings had to face the same brutal winter inside their apartment.

Can you imagine sleeping with your winter coat on? Well, the landlord's excuse was that the boiler was broken, and that he was working on it. What a character! I can still remember him, with a big cigar hanging out the side of his mouth. Every time he spoke to Mom, he was wearing a black cashmere coat and a hat tilted to the side, wearing his glasses. Mom had to deal with this drama king because Dad was sleeping after a long night's work. This meant Mom had to heat hot water for the entire family to wash up. It was very organized. I don't remember my siblings, my parents or I fighting about this routine. This boiler drama went on for years on and off. The only time we fought was for the bathroom. Imagine having only one bathroom for six people. When you must go, you must go. Many times, Mom used to say, "Cut the rope" if you were in the restroom and needed to get out.

My parents never complained about this situation to the point that it affected us. I believe we understood our parents' frustration—trapped in a 6th-floor tenement building, with garbage in the yard, behind the stairs, and some outside in front of the building about to bust out of tin garbage cans. As a matter of fact, I really don't remember seeing the garbage truck a lot. I guess they seldom came around, or I don't recall.

Besides the cold nights in the winter, we had to sometimes fend off rats the size of cats that made their way into human dwelling places.

Speaking of rats, one night, there was a rat in our apartment in the middle of the night. We screamed for our parents. My father grabbed the broom, and the rat stood on its hind legs to confront him. The rest is a blur to me, but my dad got rid of it.

It did not matter how clean your apartment was because some of your neighbors may have left dirty dishes in their sink, forgot to take out their trash, or even just been a pig. To make matters worse, there was also garbage in the backyard from some tenants in two buildings.

It is amazing how I can still remember these snippets of memories in the ghetto from my formative years till this day. Little did I know that I would bring my own children to places of my humble beginnings to memorialize the struggles of success.

Ecclesiastes 3:1, *A Time for Everything:* *"There is a time for everything, and a season for every activity under the heavens:"*

2. Puerto Rico

In the early 1960s, as well as the late 1960s, women were in the workforce but were second-class citizens, from my point of view—at home too. Men dominated the workforce and the household. Perhaps this may not be true for some women from the '60s, but in a Hispanic household, you were not to voice your opinion unless asked. This kept the peace in the house. Mami always, throughout my entire life, shared that when a man is hot under the collar, you are not to speak. You should wait for his anger to dissipate, and then he will listen. In other words, your husband can get angry, but you can't.

During the winter of 1963, we took a trip to Puerto Rico to meet our grandfather from Mami's side of the family. We stayed at our Uncle Cheo and Titi Ana's house. Although my memory is foggy, I remember my Uncle Cheo as a despot. I remember sitting on a big chair, and Uncle Cheo asking me why I had nail polish on my nails, and on top of that, he said, "Be sure to cross your legs when you sit in a chair." For crying out loud, I was only 6 years old and very sensitive since I was the middle child and sort of did not fit in. I still used to wet the bed at times and got into a lot of trouble for that. We did not stay at *tío* Cheo's house because Mami had a disagreement with him, and all of us had to leave to Grandpa's house, where there was less room. This did not surprise me at all.

When we arrived at *Abuelo and Abuela's* house, they were so welcoming. Grandma was not my mother's biological mother, so they were not the best of friends because Mom was a tough teenager when *Abuelo* married her. Her mother passed away when she was only eighteen months old. Mami told me about all the mischief she was involved in when she occasionally lived with her dad and stepmom Margarita. Mami was raised from house to house because Grandpa had to work. She was sometimes with her great *tía, aunt* Gila or her grandmother Marcelina. My **Titi** used to tell me that when Mami was little, she did not want her around because she would mess up her dolls. Apparently, my Titi spent more time with Grandma Marcelina than Mom.

On other occasions, Titi also told me that when Abuelo had to take Titi and Mami home, Mami was always too tired or pretended to be asleep, and he would have to carry her all the way home while Titi walked.

Anyway, we stayed for about two weeks. Puerto Rico is a beautiful Island with flowers, tropical creatures—especially el Coqui, with its magical singing at night, and the sounds of the rooster Cock A Doodle Doo early in the morning. You do not need an alarm clock.

One day, our family went to visit one of my mother's aunts. We were either having a late lunch or an early dinner. I remember a long kitchen table where we all sat, ready to be served. Everything looked delicious. It was fresh chicken from the backyard. I believe I asked Mami what that meant. She said that my aunt had chickens in her backyard. All she had to do was kill one, and that's what's on the table. That was it! I did not eat, and my siblings, having heard the same thing, did not eat. Of course, Mami encouraged us, and we ate some, but the thought of killing a hen did not sit well with us.

I remember returning to my first-grade class on a cold day. My parents took me to school to talk to my teacher and talked about our family trip. I would say this: when I realized that there was a world outside of 323 East 108 Street in East Harlem, I began to dream!

Romans 12:18, *"If it is possible, as far as it depends on you, live at peace with everyone."*

3. Communion

There were a lot of interesting events going on in the United States in 1964. President Lyon B. Johnson signed the Civil Rights Act that would be the beginning of more Civil Rights Acts to follow for equality. In boxing, Muhammed Ali won the Heavyweight Championship against Sonny Liston in February 1964. The Beatles arrived in New York City from John F. Kennedy Airport, and Beatlemania began in the United States with rock and roll. In Hollywood, Sidney Poitier won the best actor award in Santa Monica, California. Religious beliefs were very important in our society.

Learning about one's faith and learning to speak English was very common in the 1960s.

Titi was very concerned about us because Mami only spoke to us in Spanish and was concerned about our religious education.

Since we were Catholic, Titi wondered why we had not done our communion, one of the sacraments of the Catholic Church. She did not want us being raised like the heathen, who did not know God. My father, by then, had already converted to another faith and did not agree with Mami's religious practices or her beliefs. Since Mami did not work, she could not send us to religious instruction because, at the end of the religious classes, she would not be able to purchase the clothes my sister and I would need for our communion. Dad was not going to pay for it. He did not agree with Mami at all.

Mami, suddenly, developed tough skin, and she was not having it. She decided to go to work at a factory in Queens just for the communion expenses. My brother, Hector, was not old enough yet. You had to be 7 years old.

We were enrolled in religious classes at Saint Anne's Church in Spanish Harlem. As I recall, children in public school were dismissed early for religious instruction. I remember lining up every Wednesday in the school hallway in public school while the classroom teachers ensured that students enrolled in religious instruction left on Wednesdays at about 2:15 p.m. with the people responsible for them. Parents did not have to worry about picking up their children until after the religious instruction class in the afternoon at the church. I still remember the nuns teaching lessons about being good Christians and taking us inside the church to show us what to do during a ceremony.

Spring was around the corner, and we had met the requirements for communion.

Our communion day was so special! Mami styled our hair and made herself our official hairdresser. After the religious ceremony, Mami took us for professional photos at Rene Studio on East 116 Street in Spanish Harlem near *La Marqueta,* the market where we normally shopped for clothes. Let me put it this way: Mami purchased everything at this place, except the kitchen sink. You might as well call *La Marqueta* the Puerto Rican Market!

Mami loved this newfound financial independence when she got a job at a factory. She enjoyed shopping for us and buying house goods to make our home cozier. Alexander's, Korvettes, and Gimbels were some of the other department stores where Mami loved to shop for our clothes. She really enjoyed buying us beautiful dresses, nice pants, and shirts for my brothers. After that, Mami never stopped working. Throughout her life, she would mention, "I went to work to buy your communion dresses, and I ended up working for life."

Little did she know that Papi would expect her to contribute to the household so that he could send more money to his family in Cartagena, Colombia. This did not sit well with Mami. After all, we lived in the *slums,* and she wanted a better living situation. Papi's family thought we were swimming in money. He sent money every month.

As I mentioned before, Mami worked for almost the rest of her life and did not really enjoy the fruits of her labor.

Proverbs 22:6, *"Start children off on the way they should go and even when they are old, they will not turn from it."*

4. My Kitchen Window

The late sixties were sort of a cultural revolution. There were a lot of house parties. Cigarette smoking, teased hair, and heavy make-up was very popular among young women. Young girls wanted to look like Twiggy, the model from England. Women wore mini-skirts, and men wore long hair. There were also hippies. Some people called this period the British invasion because of new singing groups like the Beatles and the Rolling Stones, who arrived at our shores.

Our ghetto apartment in Harlem was cozy and very clean. Mami and Papi both worked to make ends meet. There was no junk food at home, and welfare was a no-no. As far as my parents were concerned, you had to work and not depend on the government, unless it was necessary.

School was fun! We had so many school friends, and our neighborhood was a community of families that helped each other.

The late '60s was a time when many Puerto Ricans moved to New York City. You know how it is. When you move, all your extended family decides to move to the same country, or area, or maybe the same street block or building.

I remember being eight years old and the birthday party my mama had for me with our neighbors in the sixth-floor apartment. I hated cake but loved the ice cream. House parties were very common in the sixties.

Our family was very close-knit. Since Mami and Papi worked, they had to pay for babysitters. We were four children—two boys, and two girls. My youngest brother was at least two. My sister did not want to have anything to do with babies, especially changing soiled diapers and having to wash them.

My youngest brother was so cute, and I especially loved to care for him. This meant changing his diapers when he was born. I was only six years old when he was born. It did not matter because I knew what to do. Mami fired the babysitter because we told her we did all the work, and all she did was sit and watch television. This meant I had to prepare my little brother's bottle and change his soiled diapers. As a matter of fact, I helped Mami all the time. If the neighbor had a baby, I would help also.

My mother was so proud of us. She knew that we would never open the door to anyone. Furthermore, Fannie, the Italian woman next door, knew we were alone because she and Mami came to an agreement that we would knock on her door in case of an emergency.

Mami always said that she was so proud of how we cared for each other. Sometimes, she would comment, "Elsie, you love children so much that I worry that you will not have any. Your sister will probably end up with all the kids since she does not like them much." People were very superstitious in that era. I really believed it too!

Although I was just a child, this really left a lasting impression on my inner soul. Mami made this comment many times to me or mentioned it to my aunt or friends. For some reason, being as inquisitive as I normally was, I began to ask myself questions or even worry about this. I decided I had to talk to somebody about this situation that burned inside of me. I wanted to grow up one day and raise a family like Mami. Who would I talk to? Besides, I was a child and thought Mami would think I was silly to worry about such a thing.

One night, I was alone in my kitchen. I had no idea where the rest of the family was at that moment. I do remember that it was dark outside, and the stars were out, even though my kitchen fluorescent light was on. That night, I decided to look up into the night sky and talk to God. I said, "Are the children I will bear one day in the sky waiting to be born? I wonder, God. How many will I have? I know, God, that they must be in heaven, waiting to be born. I know that one day, in the future, You will send them down from heaven to be born. It's just not time, right, God?"

Eighteen years later, at the age of twenty-six, I had my first daughter, Angela. She was an angel! When I turned twenty-eight, I was blessed with another bundle of joy, Genevieve, my second daughter. Twelve years later, my first son, Angelo, was born, and my last son, Marcel, was born three months before my forty-third birthday. God did hear my prayer, the prayer of a child who had the faith to believe that all things were possible. As a child, I had no doubt. I must remind myself that if Jesus heard me then, He still hears me today. "Now faith is the substance of things hoped for, the evidence of things not seen." That night, I truly believed that all my children were in heaven, waiting to be born.

Hebrews 11:1 (KJV), *"Now faith is the substance of things hoped for, the evidence of things not seen."*

5. Hop In, Kid!

It was about 1965, and our school usually had parent and teacher shows. They were very interested in building the school community. This brought the community together into a school setting for fun and laughter. The audience was always packed. It was an event parents, teachers, and students did not want to miss.

When I was in elementary school, I enjoyed music so much. However, I couldn't join the choir until 5th grade. In the meantime, all other students, like myself, who were below 5th grade, had music lessons with recorders. There was singing in class and reading simple counts in music. This was not the choir, but my teacher did have us perform at least one choir piece on Christmas. The piece was "I Remember Mommy Kissing Santa Claus" by Michael Jackson and the Jackson 5.

Fast forward, during one hot summer day in 1967, one of our teachers gave us a choice of a homework assignment in class. We had to either recite a poem or sing a song. I thought to myself, *I am not reciting a poem; it's too hard to memorize a poem overnight. Singing a song, I know, will be easier.*

I sang my song "Moon River." Suddenly, I was asked to report to the assistant principal's office, Mr. Phillips.

I thought I was in big trouble. They asked me to sing, and I did; the next thing you know, I was sent from class to class. I was like a little novelty. Singing was my outlet, and I never thought anything about it because it was my hobby in Spanish, and now in English. However, I was more comfortable singing in Spanish.

One Saturday morning, a music teacher showed up at our ghetto apartment on the 6th floor. He spoke to my parents about me taking piano lessons downtown at a reasonable price. My father agreed to take me.

Within a month or so, my father took me somewhere downtown for my first piano lesson. Going downtown was a big thing. I was overcome by the big billboards, the hustle and bustle of people, and the huge signs. I felt lost in such a large city. This area of downtown was new for me. Besides Puerto Rico, I had not seen so much, except for Radio City Music Hall with Mom, who saved every penny to take us to see the Rockets and Santa Claus.

When we arrived, he spoke to someone in charge. Dad said that he would pick me up after my lesson. I sat and sat, and no one inquired about me. Somehow, there was some misunderstanding. When a lady came to the front desk to call the next client, it was not my name. This made me curious, so I approached her and asked her about my lesson. She said that I wasn't scheduled until the following Saturday. No one else said a word to me, but perhaps they thought I would wait for my dad.

I walked out of the studio as if I knew where to go. I became mesmerized by New York City streets, people, traffic, and the signs plastered all over the place. I guess I walked too far and did not know in which direction to walk to return to the studio. I had to think fast. What could I do? The traffic seemed to catch my attention, and so I decided to step off the sidewalk and hail a cab. What was I thinking?

A big yellow medallion cab stopped. Behind the wheel was this big Caucasian lady, about 300 pounds, blond hair to her shoulders, wearing a dress. She said, "What's the matter, kid?" I said, "Miss, I am lost. I was supposed to have a piano lesson today, but I guess my dad got the dates mixed up. I walked out of the studio, and now I do not know where it is." The lady took one look at me and said, "Hop in, kid. Where do you live?" I said, "323 East 108 street." She drove me all the way home and said, "Be careful." Before exiting the cab, I held out my hand and offered the cabbie the only money I had, fifteen cents. She said, "Keep the change, kid." I was safe! As I think about this experience in my early years, I know that the hand of God was in my life, looking after me, because He had a special job for me. I would be a teacher one day, and this meant souls for the Lord. **No child should ever do what I did.** It is very dangerous, but God protected me.

Genesis 28:15, *"I will not leave you until I have done what I have promised you."*

6. Italian Feast

The 1960s was a wild time in the United States. Women wore heavy make-up, teased their hair, wore Go-go boots and miniskirts. There was The Woodstock Rock Festival and musical hits like "In the Ghetto" by Elvis Presley and "The Age of Aquarius" by The Fifth Dimension. Neil Armstrong was the first man to walk on the moon.

Life at East 108 Street was exciting during the summer months. There was entertainment, and I would dare to say that this went on the entire summer.

The Saint Anthony Italian Feast in East Harlem was every summer and ended around Labor Day on East 108 Street between 1st and 2nd Avenue. I don't exactly remember if the preparation started at the end of June or the beginning of July. I do know that it was the most electrifying time on my block. You see, I lived at 323 East 108 Street, where there was a shrine that was built next to my apartment building. This meant that after a church mass, the Saint Antonio statue was carried from the church through the streets, with a long procession and a live band playing. The statue had large amounts of dollar bills on it and was placed in the shrine.

In preparation for the feast, men had to build a tall structure made of wood that reached up to my 6th-floor apartment. After they finished building the wooden structure, they hung religious figures of the Catholic Faith. It sort of reminded me of a totem pole.

This religious structure also included a platform that was used to accommodate the band and the singer while about 60 men carried it. Singing was done in Italian, and it was beautiful! They danced the structure up and down the block and from side to side while the band played, and the singer sang. In front of the procession was a bandleader who directed the men with the structure. The men wore white pants, a white shirt, red berets, and a white or red scarf around their necks. This was serious business!

Besides the Italian Totem Pole, a carousel, the Hammer ride, a merry-go-round, and other rides that I cannot remember were being built for the carnival during the day and evenings. The feast had games, Italian sausages, Italian ices, and Zeppoles were cooked in a deep oil fryer. This is a sweet dough that is fried, and then powdered sugar is used as a topping.

The evenings were great because it seemed as if the feast continued at least until 9:00 p.m. or 10:00 p.m. My siblings and I used to do everything in the apartment so that Mami would not have to cook or clean the house. This meant we would have dinner when Mami came home, and then she would take us outside. She usually sat across the street on a Franklin Plaza bench while we were at the feast on the street. It was so much fun!

The Italian feast had a surprise, as far as I was concerned. You see, there was also another stage constructed on the block facing my apartment building. It was an opera show! I remember tables in the street, with people dressed up. It looked like a black-tie affair. It was like the shows you see on television televised from Italy, with people dressed up being served food and drinks. This affair was no joke! When the orchestra started, a woman was introduced in Italian, and then she sang. I heard opera for the first time. I laughed but thought, *what could she be singing?* I was interested! It was as if a piece of Italy was planted right in front of 323 East 108 Street apartment building that evening as my family and I watched and listened to the opera from our 6th-floor fire escape for free.

I must admit that these Italian feasts were so exciting! Little did I know that I would fall in love with the opera. Between the opera on my block once a year and Handel's Messiah for school shows, I learned to appreciate a different musical world. No matter how poor we were, we were blessed. This had no price tag! It is learning to appreciate what you have instead of focusing on what you don't have or the state you live in. This includes the frozen winters with no heat, and the rats we had to fend off in the middle of the night. These experiences helped me dream of a better life for future generations, including mine.

This is the American Dream!

Philippians 4:11–13, *"[11] I am not saying this because I am in need, for I have learned to be content whatever the circumstances. [12] I know what it is to be in need, and I know what it is to have plenty. I have learned the secret of being content in any and every situation, whether well fed or hungry, whether living in plenty or in want. [13] I can do all this through him who gives me strength."*

Chapter Three

1. Across the Hall

During the late 1960s, drugs were becoming more obvious in the streets of Harlem. Regardless of who you were, you were affected. It was a scary time because drug abuse was talked about behind closed doors in the privacy of your home. Some students in school were addicted to drugs, and some even overdosed. People wanted to move, but jobs were hard to come by. Puerto Rican people had a difficult time because many did not speak English or were resistant to learning it. There were some who did and were able to obtain better employment. At least, in some cases, that is what I witnessed.

Around 1968, we were moving, finally! Guess what? Our new place would be the apartment next door, a few steps across the hall. We spent the entire day moving and hooking up the place. There was basically no packing, except for the kitchen and bathroom items.

Now, this meant that we would have occupied three apartments in the building by now at 323 East 108 Street. Our first apartment was a one-bedroom on the second or third floor. The second had two bedrooms, and the third had three. My parents occupied one bedroom, my sister and I another, and my brothers had a bedroom on the left side entrance of the apartment. Our rent was now $62.00.

It was around this time we were able to afford a telephone. Now, this was moving up in life—if you had a telephone at home. The ringing was so loud; Mami and Papi were the only ones authorized to use it. Later, this would change. Mami made it clear that every time you pick up the receiver, it's **chin- chin** for the telephone company, and less for our pockets. This valuable information kept us in check.

The apartment across the hall had its benefits. It faced the street, and we could see the Franklin Plaza Cooperative Buildings and its huge park. Our parents could see us in full view at the park from the sixth-floor window. This meant if you were at the park, in the basketball court section, I believe a handball court or parking lot, you could be seen.

Around dinner time, Mami would be hanging halfway out the window, yelling from the top of her lungs, "Cecilia, Elsie, Hector, Ernest, **vengan a comer**," which means "Come and eat." You could not say that you did not hear her because someone at the park, who was at a listening distance, would always inform us. My mother knew this, so there was no excuse. The Italian mothers did the same. I believe this is a cultural thing.

Climbing six flights of stairs was exhausting. Imagine climbing six flights of stairs to carry bags of food from the supermarket. When Papi arrived, it took an assembly line to carry the groceries, and guess what? We were it, except for Ernest, who was too little to carry heavy bags. This also included dragging the heavy shopping cart, with some items still in it.

From the sixth floor, you could have an agreement with a neighbor in the next building who had windows facing yours in the backyard to hang a clothesline. The neighbor would do the same. It was a way to save money and time in late spring, summer, and part of the autumn season. After returning from the laundromat with wet clothes, we hung them on the clothesline.

Across our apartment, you could see part of the staircase leading to the roof. This meant we sometimes saw the bad element going to the roof to do I don't know what or to do drugs. It was scary! At the beginning of our third move, we did not see this, but as months passed, there were more drugs on the streets. Dad had very serious talks with us about this matter. As a matter of fact, one of our neighbor's sons died of an overdose. We went to the wake to be reminded. "This can be you. Stay away from drugs."

The popular drugs were heroin, sunshine, marijuana, and God knows what else.

One day, Dad sat us all down and gave us the rundown about what was happening on the streets. He identified one person in our neighborhood with skin popping. He said, "A heroin addict covers his arms, even in hot weather. This is a sign of drug abuse. There are scars and/or blisters on the surface of the skin as evidence of drug abuse."

Another topic he warned us about was breaking the law. He said, "If any of you break the law or get locked up, I will not bail you out. You can rot in jail because I will not tolerate it."

As we aged, he warned us about parties. "Never leave a drink unattended. If you do, throw it out. You never know who can slip a pill or powdered drug. Watch the candies; they have drugs too. Oh, don't forget the cakes. A cake can have drugs too." I guess being Colombian gave him a lot of information about drugs.

School gave us classes about drugs using real footage. Our middle school did a terrific job informing students. They went as far as showing a real-life situation of an individual with an overdose, the withdrawal or foaming of the mouth, declaring the addict deceased, and then the morgue. I believe the name of the organization was "Scared Straight" or something like that.

Comparing society to then and now, marijuana was viewed differently. For years, students and teachers who took a drug class were informed about the side effects and damage to the brain cells. The information included becoming sterile, hungry, and depressed because the drug makes you feel good. As a matter of fact, we were informed that marijuana led to other drugs. Now, marijuana is good, and it is supposed to help people. This is a thriving industry, and people can't resist it.

A couple of years passed; I graduated from middle school and began my first year in high school. My brother Hector was in his last year of middle school, and my sister was in her second year of high school.

One summer day, my sister and I walked up six flights of stairs to our apartment and found ourselves with two men sitting on the staircase leading to the roof. They were burning a drug on a spoon with a cigarette lighter, a rubber wrapped around one of their arms, and a syringe, ready to inject themselves. We opened our apartment door quickly without freaking out and closed it immediately.

When Mami arrived, my sister and I told her what we saw, and she said, "It is time to move out."

However, we would not move out for two or three years. My father loved paying $62.00 for rent.

Proverbs 3:5-6
"⁵ *Trust in the Lord with all your heart and lean not on your own under-standing;*
⁶ *In all your ways submit to him, and he will make your paths straight."*

Proverbs 22:6
"Start children off on the way they should go, and even when they are old, they will not turn from it."

2. Another World

In 1969, Nixon was president of the United States, and the average salary was about $9,400. The most popular jobs were: doctor, lawyer, pilot for men, and teacher for women. The Mets won the World Series, and the average price on a gallon of milk was about $1.10.

It was the summer of 1969 when Dad planned a family trip to his hometown in South America. Even though we lived in the slums, Dad just knew how to make a dollar give birth; a math whiz he was on budgets and numbers. My family took a long vacation to Cartagena, Colombia, in the town of Canapote. We landed in Barranquilla and had to take a bus before heading to Cartagena. We entered customs with ease because the workers at the airport had been educated by my grandfather, and so, this was a way of thanking him. Apparently, there was no direct flight, or perhaps it was too expensive. Our derrières were not even planted on seats when Grandpa began questioning Mami about how much money Dad earned and how much she earned. This was the first time he met Mami, and he was asking her for information about the income in our household? My father was sitting with my brothers, so he could not possibly listen in on the conversation. I happened to be sitting right in front of them. I thought, *My goodness! Doesn't he know how we live? Now, I understand why Dad is always sending money.* The American dollar is seen as wealth. This is one reason why Mom and Dad were always at odds.

It was a great experience to see another part of the world and how others lived. Some people lived in humble houses or even huts. Little children came out into the streets in their birthday suits to jump in the rain because it was so hot! This was the norm. However, there was a huge problem; it did not matter if you wore jeans or a simple pair of sneakers. To the townspeople, you were a Yankee. This is what they called us because we came from America. As a matter of fact, when the maid took me to the marketplace, a black and white photo was taken of us. I didn't even notice. Anyway, the photographer showed up at my grandpa's house, inquiring about purchasing the photo. Even though grandpa had two teenagers as household help, it did not mean he was wealthy; these young girls earned their keep, and they were related to us in some way.

Grandpa had purchased a goat that we named America and a dog—I don't remember his name. We also had the opportunity to ride a donkey and visit friends of the family who lived in a hut. These people prepared the most delicious meal cooked on coals in pots. You did not need a gourmet kitchen to whip up a delicious meal.

Since we were expected at Grandpa's house, my dad had to send money to build a bathroom. His family was still using an outhouse before my dad sent money. There was a schoolhouse next to the house, a few steps away. The front of the house had a huge sign that read, "The Madrid Property." There was a tall brick wall that surrounded the property as well. Grandma Catalina said that it deterred thieves from stealing the hens or the eggs in the morning. Although Catalina was not my biological grandmother, she was kind and loving. She held class outside the schoolhouse while I sat on her lap, and the students listened attentively. When they were in the schoolhouse, everyone behaved. Education was no joke in this school. At night, my grandpa held an English class for adult learners.

Colombians are very cheery, hospitable people; they love music, dancing, and drinking. Grandpa threw a party to honor Dad. There was music, conversations, and dance.

One of my grandpa's neighbors did not have any children and just fell in love with my youngest brother Ernest. Ernest would get up in the morning to knock on the neighbor's door for breakfast, with a baby bottle in his hand for Colombian coffee. I could not believe it. My brother knew how much he was loved. The couple had not been able to conceive, so Ernest was their temporary son.

One day, Ernest untied the dog and took him to the marketplace. Although Ernest was only six years old, he was fearless. We realized he was missing and freaked out. The neighbors came to tell us because they had seen him at the marketplace with the dog. Dad ran to get him.

My aunt Mercedes, my father's half-sister, took us to school with her in the late morning. We had a very heavy breakfast, and when we got to her high school, she bought us a very cold oatmeal drink that tasted delicious.

At least three or four weeks passed, and it was time to go home. My father had his third cousin, whose name is Mercedes, purchase our airline tickets. She was supposed to get us a bargain, being that she worked for an airline. We said our goodbyes. The neighbors next door came and said a special goodbye to Ernest.

We took a cab and made it to the airport. As we exited the cab, the driver tried to leave us behind without our luggage. Thank God Mami was watching him. My Dad found out that his cousin got so much of a bargain that we had to return to Grandpa's house. There were good intentions, but it didn't pan out that way. For the first time, I heard my father curse underneath his breath. This was a lesson for me. **"Lo barato sale caro."** This means that cheap is expensive. My third cousin only did as she was asked. It was not her fault.

Now, when we were at Grandpa's house again, he was trying to convince my dad to let Mami travel alone with us to the United States, and that later, he would follow. My sweet grandma Catalina sensed what was happening and adamantly said, "If the family came together, they must leave together." I was suspicious about this idea too. Was Grandpa trying to separate Mami and Dad?

The next day, we said our last goodbyes and left. My father and my brother Hector would return for at least two or three summers before Grandpa passed away.

1 Timothy 6:10, *"For the love of money is the root of all kinds of evil. By craving it, some have wandered away from the faith and pierced themselves with many sorrows."*

3. Hail to Jefferson Park

The late 1960s and the early 1970s had significant events. The Civil Rights Act of 1964 put an end to segregation in public places. The 1969 census reported 24 million people living in poverty. Earth Day was celebrated for the first time on April 22, 1970, with millions of Americans demonstrating their concerns for keeping the environment clean.

By September of 1969, I began middle school in Spanish Harlem at 240 East 109 Street and 3rd Avenue then named Jefferson Park Middle School or I. S 117.

The two years spent at Jefferson Park were AMAZING! Many of my successes and talents were discovered and nurtured at this school. My first memory of this school is changing classes, and the hallways flooded with students rushing to class. It was an organized mob. Unfortunately, someone was curious about me and grabbed my butt in the middle of the hallway. I couldn't see who it was because there were so many students. I was so hysterical that one of my teachers, Mr. Settle, tried to calm me down, and he did. Since I did not see who grabbed me, there was no sense in pursuing an investigation. Anyway, I realized that I could not identify the pervert and decided to get over it.

Jefferson Park had a wonderful curriculum that included the arts and sciences. I say this because there was biology, social studies, shop, sewing, cooking, band and orchestra, drama, choir, and art. We learned real-life skills and were immersed in the arts. Let me put it this way: the art, music, and choir worked together for all fall, winter, spring, and summer shows being presented in the evening for parents and students. I believe these events and preparations led to community building.

I was automatically programmed for violin with Mr. Bernard. I believe that was his name. What a sweet and kind teacher. I just did not want to learn about any string instrument. The choir was my biggest interest. Just to cut to the chase, since Papi worked nights, I had him come in to have my program changed. I know there was an audition for choir because I was placed in the alto section. Singing was my thing. However, although I loved the popular music of the time, like the Carpenters, The Jackson 5, The Temptations, The Supremes, and more, singing in Spanish was my passion. After all, my parents loved music, especially Papi. He played all types of music that included classical. I remember Papi trying to engage my siblings and myself in identifying some of the instruments played in Peter and the Wolf music; I remember that the flute represented the bird.

Choir was a very interesting class. Ms. Purdy was our music teacher who played a mean piano and could really sing. She also had an assistant music teacher who was very knowledgeable and played the piano when Ms. Purdy had her eyes completely on the choir. Singing was serious business at this school! If you were illiterate, you learned how to read quickly.

We learned our music pieces by first listening and repeating the words of the song without a text or music sheet. These words were presented in the way one would sing them when you were ready to sing them with the accompaniment of the piano. However, it was a process. Listen to the words, repeat the words. Sing the words with the score sheet for counting, rests, crescendos, decrescendo, staccatos, and more. So, illiteracy went out the window. The words committed to memory were then connected to a text you already had in your head. How can you lose?

There was always some kind of theme and competition for solos. This means you had to try out in front of the music teacher and sometimes the band teacher. There were no complaints about how someone may have had two solos. You either had it or not.

There was one problem for me. I did not want to sing my solos in English. I did not feel comfortable. For Puerto Rican Discovery Day, I was selected to sing a solo and asked Ms. Purdy if I could sing my song in Spanish, and her response was, "If you can tell me in English what you are going to sing in Spanish, you may sing it." This began my crossover journey from Spanish to English. I remember one of our Christmas shows because it included Handel's Messiah. Little did I know that Ms. Purdy had shared the gospel without saying a word.

For another performance, we had an African theme, and all students went to Harlem to get their dashiki dresses or shirts and an African head-wrap for the girls made at a special store Ms. Purdy recommended. We were taught to sing an African lullaby, ***Bayeza ku sa sa*** ... It was an amazing performance. There was community and sensitivity for other cultures. We also had students from Taiwan, who were recent arrivals, who were part of the choir and learned how to embrace their new homeland, America.

By the end of the 7th grade, I began singing solos in English. Rehearsals for the choir were at 8:00 a.m. One morning, we were singing ***I'd Like to Teach the World to Sing in Perfect Harmony***, and some of my choir classmates decided they would change the song. Instead of singing "I'd like to build a world a home and furnish it with love ..." they sang "I'd like to build a world a home and furnish sh_t with love ..." Ms. Purdy stopped the singing and said, "It is not furnish sh_t with love but furnish it with love." She was not having it. After this episode, no one in the choir dared to fool around during choir practice.

I remember one day when Ms. Purdy modeled for me how to walk and present myself in public and how to work the stage. We were alone in the auditorium when she said, "You hold the microphone like this; you walk like this; you look straight at the clock, and it will seem as if you are looking at the audience." What a mentor!

After one performance, Ms. Purdy invited parents and students from the choir to her condo apartment. The day before, Ms. Purdy and I had prepared fried chicken and other foods for this party. Performances were standing-room-only in the auditorium. I would say the entire community attended. The choir was accompanied by the orchestra and the band; it was spectacular! The art department also collaborated with the stage and auditorium scenery. Sometimes the choir, orchestra, and band members were involved too. It seems to me that we were allowed two electives. The school was ahead of its time in technology. Students grew in front of the camera. My solos were filmed, and you could see that the first films showed me singing in Spanish. I do not remember the rest, but I would not be surprised if they have these films in the basement of the school somewhere.

Besides the choir, band, and orchestra, there was a sewing class. Students learned how to cut a pattern; follow the instructions; select a fabric for a skirt, vest, or dress. You were graded on this project. Every student, from what I recall, had access to a Singer Sewing Machine.

Nutrition was taught in cooking class, and we had a couple of stoves. Although there were other recipes, the recipe I remember is applesauce. A big bulletin board outside this classroom caught my attention. It was about how early nutrition affects your body in a positive way, especially long before the childbearing years. It is astonishing how a bulletin board made such an impression on me. It must be that the contents learned in class were displayed in a public setting.

Drama was another elective many students joined. They also had performances, and the teacher was always open to any performance students wanted to present. I remember a show on pantomimes. The audience was really engaged and was packed again with parents, teachers, and students.

For my sister's 8th grade graduation, our choir band and orchestra played "Let the Sunshine In" by the Fifth Dimension. I was the soloist, and guess what happened? The microphone stopped working. I said to myself, "The show must go on." I decided to dance around the stage as the orchestra played and the choir continued singing. The audience thought it was all part of the act.

We are all born with a gift. It is not ours to keep. Later in life, I would sing in a choir, teach language in the classroom through music, sing to my four children before bed or during their baths. It is a gift that can call people to Christ. You do not have to be a professional singer or be famous to make a mark in this world. Music is a universal language that can transcend in a spiritual way. Music is the language that can teach a child to read. Reading is a precious gift because then you can read the word of God. Find your gift if you have not. You would be surprised "because little becomes much when you place it in the Master's Hands."

Middle School was a blast!

Isaiah 64:8, *"Yet you, Lord, are our Father. We are the clay, you are the potter; we are all the work of your hand."*

4. Thirteen

History was made when the voting age was lowered from 21 to 18 during Nixon's presidency. Rock and roll and disco music were very popular and successful. The Spanish channel was extremely popular with the Hispanic community. There were **Novelas** like "Simplemente Maria" (**Simply Maria)** and **"Esmeralda"** (Emerald). The protagonists for both soap operas were Jose Bardina and Lupita Ferrer.

During my middle school years from 1969–1972, school wasn't the only place I had extracurricular activities. There was another thing to do. The Borough Youth Choir was on Saturday mornings downtown. Students had to audition for this choir, and I was part of it.

My next-door neighbors had a great influence on my parents. We had a family next door from the Dominican Republic. They had two sons Alex and Walter who attended school with me. They also had an aunt living with them, who was studying to be a nurse and learning English too. She used a record player to learn English. Our neighbor's husband was a hard-working man who did not want his wife to help him financially. One day, she knocked on our door, crying for help. I do not know what her husband was thinking, but she was employed at a factory he knew nothing about. Somehow, she wanted support from my parents to verify that she was working. Perhaps Mami put in a word for her at her job, and so, that would make Mami her alibi that she was nowhere else. Walter and Alex's mother also took out some paperwork to verify employment. As a result, our families became good friends.

One night the boys, who attended school with me, wanted to go to one of the school's evening performances to hear me sing because I had a solo that night. I believe Walter and Alex were given permission to attend since they went with Mami and my siblings. After the performance, the boys told their parents about it and how my solo went.

One day, our neighbors informed my parents about **Noche de Aficionado los miércoles**—amateur night every Wednesday at around 7:00 or 7:30 p.m. They thought it would be a great opportunity to put my name out there to become a professional singer. Mami loved the idea. I would say that about two weeks later, I was one of the singers at the theater. Mom spoke to the people in charge of the show and found out it was free to participate.

Since Alex and Walter attended school with me, they thought I was talented enough to try my luck at this contest. It seemed to me that this was community entertainment. **Aficionado** (Amateur) means you are not a professional singer, but you sing with a live orchestra. Some contestants provided their own sheet music adapted to their voice. My parents did not have any money for this, so I had to have a good ear and sing on key. The audience paid a small fee to participate. After all, there was a live orchestra, and the people behind the contest needed to pay the announcer or master of ceremony and the orchestra. The winner of the contest was decided by the audience. The louder the claps, the better it was to eliminate those contestants whose claps were lower. It was evident that if you had more guests sitting in the audience, this meant you would get more claps. More clapping meant you had a greater chance of winning and then moving on to the next round.

These competitions went on for weeks. This meant that every week, you needed a new song and needed to be ready for the accompaniment of the orchestra. This process was like "friendo y comiendo." In Puerto Rico and the Dominican Republic, this phrase means right away, quickly—like the literal meaning, cooking and eating at the same time.

A final competition would be presented in **El Teatro Puerto Rico**. The Puerto Rican Theatre was located at 490 East 138 Street in the Bronx. This meant that every Wednesday, there was a rehearsal. I remember my mother stating that all the parents of the contestants had to sell tickets to family and friends. In other words, we had to pack the auditorium. My dad did not want me to compete. He didn't know that Mom purchased a dress for me for every Wednesday show before the final competition and now sold tickets in the neighborhood, at work, and to the family to pack the auditorium for the finale—meaning the final competition.

Competitors for the amateur night on Wednesdays were of all ages, males, females, and children. People were more partial to the children. We sang all the Spanish hits by Hispanic artists of the day. Just to name a few: Camilo Sesto, Rafael, Sandro, Jose-Jose, Yolandita Monje, Nidia Caro, Rocio Durcal, Angela Carrasco, Ednita Nazario, and others.

Competition night was exciting! My extended family like Titi, friends, including Dad and my Colombian side of the family, came to see the show. I will never forget the dress Mami purchased in Alexander's Department Store. The dress was a very light-colored lilac snug to my waist. There were white fake diamond buttons that divided the tightly snuggled upper portion of the sleeveless dress from the middle of the dress. The rest of the dress, from the waist down, had thin pleats. I felt like a goddess! I can still remember this dress.

I looked around backstage to see what other contestants were doing. I remember a female contestant in her thirties with her singing coach practicing some notes. In another section, a male in his twenties was fixing his collar and tie. The other contestants, except for a nine-year-old, were teenagers like me. It was a tough competition. The twenty-year-old male won the contest. The event and its contestants were publicized, I believe, in *El Diario,* a Spanish daily newspaper for the Hispanic community. There were trophies and money as a prize for the winner.

I will never forget the applause, all the contestants, and the orchestra. For some reason, I don't know what happened to *Noche de Aficionado*—amateur night every Wednesday at around 7:00 or 7:30 p.m. It was a money-making machine for those individuals who ran the operation. It was community entertainment. It was a wonderful opportunity for young kids, like me, to take risks, discover their talents, and have great fun.

Singing would follow me for many years. I sang to my children, to my school kids for educational reasons, and in choirs; I sang solos and participated in many church events. Even after I became a mother with my first set of children, I still found time to sing in church choirs. After my second set of children, I did not return to the choir. Now that I am in the very early winter of my years, I am singing in the church choir. Praising the Lord is great. It's good for the soul.

Psalm 104: 33–34, *"I will sing to the LORD all my life; I will sing praise to my God as long as I live. May my meditation be pleasing to him, as I rejoice in the LORD."*

5. Bully

The 1970s had many memorable slogans like: "It's the real thing" (Coca-Cola), "How many licks does it take?" (Tootsie Pop) "You deserve a break today" (McDonald's), and more. The Beatles broke up as a group. "Raindrops Keep Fallin' on My Head" by B.J. Thomas made the Billboard, and the Disco ERA was around the corner.

I was in 7th grade when an 8th grader, who I did not know, started throwing ice or snowballs at me after dismissal. It was a scary experience. I did not know where my sister was because dismissal is busy, and students are all over the place. Besides, my sister could not help me even if I told her. This boy was in the 8th grade, and he was big. I perceived him this way because I was a very small and very skinny 7th grader.

I never even shared this situation with a soul. It was as if I were so scared that it paralyzed me. This is what happens when you are being bullied, and the bully knows you are scared, and you won't share with someone who can help you. This went on almost the entire year. The cycle was a chase when I saw him. I had no idea what he wanted, and I was not about to find out. His face had no name, but I knew that I needed to find out. I was now too tired and afraid.

One afternoon at school, I had requested a pass from art class to go to music. I do not remember the reason, but it was important. No one was in the hallway, not even a school aide who was usually there. Guess what? The bully showed up. I have no idea where he came from. I do know that he pushed me into the door that led me to a hallway, with stairs leading up and down. He cornered me into the wall. The only thing I had to defend myself was a pen I had in my hand along with a pass. He said, "If you don't kiss me,

I will not let you go." I was freaking out and in a panic. I pulled out the pen and poked him on the shoulder, and this shocked him. He punched me on the chest and pushed me on the staircase. Since I had wooden clogs, I used my legs to push him down the stairs. This fighting, I felt, went on the entire period until the bell rang. It was my salvation because the school aides broke up the fight, and we both landed in the assistant principal's office.

I informed the assistant principal that he had been following me almost the entire year. This also included throwing ice or snowballs at me on my way home. His defense was, "She stabbed me with that pen in her hand." I said, "Of course, I poked you with the pen; you tried to force me to kiss you!"

Now, I had mustered up some guts to make this bully pay for harassing me for no reason. I told my father all about my situation, and he was furious. "Why didn't you tell me?"

The next day, Dad went to school and asked for the assistant principal. The young man was in the office when Dad arrived. He was reprimanded for bullying me. The assistant principal informed the student, "When you see Elsie on one side of the street, you better cross the street to the other side. If you don't, you will not graduate this year."

When the student left, my dad was still angry and told the assistant principal that if this young man continued to assault me, he would give me a bat to defend myself. This was his way of letting the school know that something had to be done about this situation.

Always turn to your parents for help. I was relieved for the rest of the year and was thanking God that this young man would not be terrifying me anymore. I also learned how to trust that adults like my father would help me if I would just ask.

I guess a bully is a bully until the coward decides he's not.

Matthew 7: 8–11
"⁸ For everyone who asks receives, and he who seeks finds, and to him who knocks it will be opened. ⁹ Or what man is there among you who, when his son asks for a loaf, will give him a stone? ¹⁰ Or if he asks for a fish, he will not give him a snake, will he? ¹¹ If you then, being evil, know how to give good gifts to your children, how much more will your Father who is in heaven give what is good to those who ask Him!"

6. Mami the Nurse

The nursing profession was very popular in the 1970s. I remember my neighbor who was a new arrival to the United States; she was studying nursing and English at the same time. Another friend of our family who lived across the street was already a nurse.

Teenagers may feel awkward. Sometimes, their extremities stand out, and there are blemishes or acne. I have heard some of the members on my mother's side of the family say, "Oh my goodness, my daughter is going through an ugly stage. Did you look at her?"

One summer day, Mami and I had to ride the city bus somewhere, and I could not place half of my butt on the seat. I couldn't because I had a boil the size of a breast. Mom asked, "What is wrong with you?" I said, "Mami, I have a boil that looks like a volcano ready to erupt. It is a gigantic pimple!"

Mom said, **"Cuando lleguemos a casa, enséñame esta ampolla,"** which means "When we get home, show me this boil."

After our trip, we got home, and I showed Mami my boil. She took one look at it and said, "If I take you to the doctor, they are going to have to lance it to get rid of the pus and clear the infection, and your butt will not be the same. This is what you are going to do: you are to take the hottest bath and sit in it for a while every single night before bed. The second thing I need for you to do is to sleep with a girdle and rub **belladonna** (a black type of cream used for mumps) every night. In the morning, wash up, rub *belladonna* again every day and wear the girdle. The purpose for this is to make the boil erupt or come to a head." She checked the boil every single day until she saw that the boil had started to erupt on its own. The instructions Mami gave me were: stand up, do not move, and take the pain. "I must squeeze it until it bleeds," she said. This is an indication that the infection was removed from the root. It was so painful, and Mami said, "Hold on until I'm done." It was not long, but it hurt!!! There was no scar, and I never had it again.

There were other times Mami was a nurse. Whenever I was uncomfortable with cramps, she made me a *manzanilla* tea, a tea to alleviate the pain.

There was always boric acid and an eyewash cup for the occasional stye on your eye and other remedies I do not recall. There is nothing better than a mom. She may not say she loves you with her words, but she shows you how much she loves you in her actions. Mami was a woman with a quiet spirit.

Proverbs 31:25–27
"25 She is clothed with strength and dignity; she can laugh at the days to come. 26 She speaks with wisdom, and faithful instruction is on her tongue. 27 She watches over the affairs of her household and does not eat the bread of idleness."

Chapter Four

1. Sandpiper

By 1972, hairstyles were really changing. Some people permed their hair. Others wore a layered haircut. Many teenagers used platform shoes and glitter pins on outfits as accessories. Girls used to tweeze their eyebrows into a thin brow and wore dark lipstick. The Maxi coat was very popular. It was a coat long enough to reach your ankles.

Dodge Vocational High School was a blast! I ended up in this school because the other high school I attended in Manhattan was not for me. There were too many fights and not my cup of tea. I felt as if I did not fit in. I told my parents, "If you do not remove me from this school, I will drop out!"

When my father went to register me at a local high school, one of the secretaries stated that we did not live in District 10. My father, having done his homework, informed the secretary where District 10 began and where it ended. She was dumbfounded and enrolled me into the cosmetology department because the nursing department was full. She stated that I could transfer the following semester, but I never did. I was having too much fun.

By the end of 10th grade, my cosmetology teachers thought I was a great fit for a work-study program at a real salon in Riverdale. By then, I knew how to deal with customers, wash hair, and manicure nails. I also learned something very vital about the salon business—I see no evil, I hear no evil, and I speak no evil. Customers stopped asking me personal questions about other clients because my response was "I don't know." Sometimes, clients would say, "I know you know but won't tell me." My response was always "If you know this, then why do you ask?" The line of questioning would stop.

Customers at the time were Irish and Jewish. They were great tippers. I was the only person of color. I was pampered and treated well by my boss and her mom who came every Saturday to get her hair done.

Saturdays and holidays were very busy, and I had no time to eat. By this time, I was about 15 but still very young at heart. I would get upset, and Nancy, my boss' mom, would run to the deli to pick up cold cuts and bread to make me a sandwich. This was the only way I could continue working. Mc Donald's was across the street, and sometimes, this was an option.

When I turned 16, the salon celebrated my birthday with gifts and a very beautiful bathing suit. My boss would say, "You cannot get married until you are 25."

One Thursday or Friday, I came to work and met a new employee. She was at least 65–70 years of age. She was hired by my boss to wash hair and manicure. However, there was a hairdresser, who worked at one of the booths, who befriended this new employee.

When new customers came in, Katie, the new employee, would say something to the client, and then I was not able to put my hands on them. The hairdresser at the booth did the same. This happened for a while.

I came up with my own remedy to help myself in this terrible situation. Whenever a client had a headache, I would offer them Tylenol. If their feet hurt, I propped them up on a chair. Slowly, I gained the favor of customers. I loved to pamper them, wash their hair, and do their manicures.

One Saturday morning, I arrived and found that my manicuring table had been confiscated by Katie. Her manicuring table was a mess, and the lamp did not work. I did not know how to handle this, so I spoke to my boss and turned the other cheek to avoid any disagreement at all costs. I quietly took her manicuring table, cleaned it up, and asked my boss to have the lamp repaired. Now, the table I cleaned up looked better and more appealing to customers. Katie came over and tried to have me return her manicuring table. My boss stepped in and said, "You took her manicuring table, and she fixed and cleaned yours. Now, you are not getting it back. The table now belongs to her."

Katie looked like a person who was from the 3rd Reich, and so was the hairdresser who worked in one of the salon's booths. They were always speaking German in my presence.

It is amazing how God always watched over me. He didn't allow an injustice. My boss was won over by my silence and did what she needed to do to make the situation right. Katie learned to respect me and realized there were no favorites at the **Sandpiper Beauty Salon.**

Romans 12:19, *"Do not take revenge, my dear friends, but leave room for God's wrath, for it is written: 'It is mine to avenge; I will repay,' says the Lord."*

Psalm 34:4, *"Turn from evil and do good; seek peace and pursue it."*

2. Finding My Voice

In the '70s, there was a lot of Disco dancing and fashion. Every day was a fashion statement, even on a short bus ride to school. Dad had successfully transferred me to Dodge Vocational High School. Now what? *I left an academic school to attend a vocational school, and that had a price.* I didn't have to take a language class to graduate and/or another advanced math class because I had a full year of Spanish and algebra at my previous school. From what I recall, I only had to take American history, business math, gym, cosmetology, and English. Cosmetology was fun and easy.

In cosmetology, we had to practice every day. However, we also needed to learn the theory on the science of hair. In other words, we needed to know how certain chemicals affected hair. A theory book on hairdressing was a resource we used to learn about the anatomy of hair and nails. As a matter of fact, the theory book looked like a book nurses would need to read.

Friday mornings, our cosmetology class was open to the public for the day under professional supervision. We worked on outside customers. This also included other students or teachers who were not part of our program. Many customers requested permanents and hair straighteners. Facials and manicures were also available. Our instructors also had their hair done. This gave students critical practice. In other words, you better know what you're doing because the cosmetology teacher would instruct you every step of the way. I also found time to get my hair and nails done, and I was at the top of my class in the cosmetology department.

Dodge Vocational High School was a fashion statement. For some great reasons, students who had another way of expressing their unfamiliar fashion were not bullied or criticized. I, for one, did not know anything about fashion until my friend Dara, who was my traveling buddy to school on the bus, told me. She looked at me on the bus one morning and discreetly said, "Elsie, did you look at yourself in the mirror today? You're psychedelic." I had no idea what the word meant, so she told me. I thought that being neat, clean, and pressed was enough. She was so cool about it that I still laugh about it today when I think about her. From then on, I became a fashion statement. I just didn't know how to before.

When I became a senior, students were running for student government. Some of my classmates asked me to run for senior class president. They said that no one in the cosmetology department ever runs; we are the un-known. I went home that afternoon to think about it. This new adventure would take me out of my comfort zone. I spoke to a dear friend of the fam-ily who was also in high school but in another school. Together, we began to brainstorm about how I could attract voters who knew nothing about me. Now, I was going from publicly singing to public speaking. How would I introduce myself? What would be my plan? What would be the focus of my campaign? What ideas could I sell them? Josefine asked if any stu-dents at school smoked cigarettes, and I said, "Yes, a lot of them, but I don't smoke." She suggested that I use oak tag paper to make campaign pins in the shape of a circle. The tags for my campaign would each have a cigarette and mint for after a smoke.

Josefine directed me to a store where cigarettes were sold at a discount because they were stale ones. With this as an incentive, we believed they would cast a vote for me. I was fortunate that the teachers or the adminis-tration did not say a word to me.

In the meantime, there was a buzz around the school that students were interested in extending the prom dance to 1:00 a.m. or 2:00 a.m. with disco music, a Latin, and a soul band to accommodate all the students in our senior population.

Josefine had great ideas. We worked together on my campaign speech and its delivery. This information was going to be disseminated to one class at a time with the blessing of the school's administration.

I introduced myself as a student from the cosmetology department and shared the ideas that students had about the extended time requested by seniors, along with the live entertainment.

The campaign race was close! I ended up as the senior class vice president. However, shortly after, the senior class president could not keep her campaign promises because she was ill. This meant that she was not able to participate in senior activities because she was absent from school.

It was then decided by the senior class team and the senior advisor that I be named president.
The team also met with the administration and shared its plan. We stated we would raise money through sales. The administration agreed if we raised the funds for the extended time for the prom and the two live bands.

Senior sales were baking goods, and seniors were reminded to pay 50 cents for our items and not to purchase any sweets from the lunchroom. This went well, but the lunchroom staff in charge of sales in the baking department was not too happy about this.

The team also spoke to teachers, and they suggested that we have a White Elephant Sale. A White Elephant Sale is a fundraiser for a cause. This sale attracted many teachers, so they contributed items in mint condition like accessories, clothes, and anything from soup to nuts. The White Elephant Sale was advertised throughout the school with posters created by our team and student volunteers. The hours for the sales were during three lunch periods. Senior class members took turns because they needed to attend class. The sales were a success!

Spring was around the corner, and we needed to know if the administration would approve two bands and the extra hour for the prom. They said we were $200.00 short to grant us our wishes, but we worked so hard that the administration found $200.00 in their budget from the previous year to give our senior class the prom of their dreams.

The senior class advisor, with the consent of parents and the administration, escorted the senior class team to different dance clubs to audition several Latin and soul bands while they worked. We also decided that our prom events should be celebrated at the Tardis Catering facility.

Now that we had our prom on the way, the team and I conducted auditions for the senior show. Many students participated in the organization of the show and its acts. The show included comedy, dancing, different singers, commercials, and two masters of ceremony. The show was during the school day.

This senior show lasted at least three hours. We were advised to cut it short. My goodness, it was a lot of fun!!!

Days later, we had a magnificent prom, with pictures taken as you entered Tardis Catering Hall. The Latin and soul bands took turns playing in between the disco music of the time. There were speeches and special thanks for all who participated to make this special event possible for the senior class.

A prom queen and king were voted on by the students and staff. I was selected as prom queen, and I believe a student named Michael was prom king.

For the first time, I found my voice on some topics I felt strong about. Student government, collaboration, negotiation, and opinions.

Proverbs 1:5, *"Let the wise listen and add to their learning, and let the discerning get guidance."*
Proverbs 27:17, *"As iron sharpens iron, so one person sharpens another."*

3. Reality Hits!

In the mid-1970s, there was open enrollment in colleges. Open enrollment was for students who needed academic support and did not have the same opportunities for a more rigorous education. In other words, perhaps you were not ready for college and were provided with opportunities to be successful. This meant remedial instruction to catch you up.

High school graduation was at the Loew's Paradise Theater on 2403 Grand Concourse in the Bronx. The senior class team was on stage, and I was given the privilege of pronouncing the senior class graduates of 1975. Now what?

I was fortunate enough to be allowed to attend College a few blocks away from home. I had to learn how to learn. My major changed several times. I needed to focus. Finally, I met a good college advisor who got in my head. Since I worked in the school system, I really enjoyed kids and worked as an assistant teacher. I also signed up at the college for a writing coach who made me realize that I was a good writer whose mind was faster than her hand could record what I meant to say.

Surrounding myself with other students who wanted to be teachers was helpful. Since I wasn't reading regularly in high school, my academic skills were weak. Every time I did something well, I would ask myself "What did I do?" so that I could repeat the process of success. This strategy became my self-help.

My courses were in English and Spanish. Most of my Spanish was learned at home. Now, I had to hone in on academic language and building stamina. The university had many subjects to offer; some of them, I had no knowledge of, neither had I even heard the words. I knew about biology but had no knowledge of chemistry, anthropology, and others. Boy, did I have my work cut out, but I refused to give up. Since I never received language support in school, my Spanish and English were not proficient. I had to learn how to learn in both languages. I made it my business to make friends with those who were proficient in Spanish and wanted to improve speaking English.

Herbert Lehman College really prepared me for teaching. I was fortunate enough to work in a school that was on the same block as the university. This allowed me to take time to review work or finish reading before going to classes. At the time, there was an early release program on Fridays for staff members who were assistant teachers.

My long journey began. Before beginning the process of learning how to learn, I made a mess of my grades and had to drop out of college for at least three semesters. I needed to get it together. This time away from school helped me to organize my life.

Sometimes, when you are 18 years old, you think you know it all. This period really humbled me, but my experience would later help me with students later.

In the meantime, I didn't think I was smart, and I was determined to change that. I learned that going to college was not what made you smart; it was what you did with the knowledge you received that makes you smart.

I became familiar with many subjects and had a problem with others. I had to learn a lot about the fine arts. I would say to myself, "What on earth is that? Chemistry, I never heard the word before." It was not part of my culture or vocabulary. Exposure to the unknown was everything for me and being brave enough to say, "I don't know." Traveling helped me a lot. It helped me to see others' points of view of the world around them.

I did not graduate with my graduation class, but I was ready to be a teacher. It has been over 37 wonderful years in the education profession. Every hardship I faced as a student, I was able to identify. This also included pushing others into more challenging assignments but never forgetting those struggling students who needed extra support because I was facing illiteracy in my classes. This became my passion! There were silent voices in the class that I needed to identify, but I also needed to identify those who were ready for more challenging assignments or a change of program.

God blesses us with gifts. They are given to us as a loan to share, and not to keep.

1 Peter 4:10, *"Each of you should use whatever gift you have received to serve others, as a faithful steward of God's grace in its various forms."*

Chapter 5

1. Lost

Roe V. Wade was in effect since 1973 and in full effect in the late '70s. There was a lot of dancing in clubs and discotheques. Studio 54 was still going strong, with many famous celebrities attending the club.

Decisions one makes in life are usually a precursor to future events; when they are without counsel, there is no one to blame but yourself.

In the summer of 1976, I met Eddie. He was a 35-year-old attractive man whom I met at a discotheque when I was about 18. He was established and looked like a promising prospect for a husband—or so I thought. He wined and dined me, and we became very personal, to say the least. I was at a very impressionable age. What do you think happened? At the age of 19, I was **pregabutt.** I confided in a friend of mine from my early middle school years to help me with getting a pregnancy test. I was devastated when I got the results. What now? I was toasted. My friend Maribel had had an abortion and stated that I needed to get one. I said "That is out of the question" but felt trapped. Why didn't I think about an organization or something for unwed mothers at the time? One thinks they know everything until a bomb blows up in their face. This meant my parents would throw me out of the house. My father used to say, "If you or your sister ever get pregnant, you will have to leave this house." Papi, my dad, was raised in Colombia, South America, even though he was born in New York City to a Puerto Rican mother and had a Colombian father. He had a very **machista** type of mentality in every sense of the word! When I found out, I told Eddie, but he had just purchased what looked like a million-dollar home in Orange County. You could say it was a mansion. He said that he was beginning his life and did not want to have this child. He worked for a firm as a researcher for attorneys. I wondered how he had mustered up so much money to buy such a place. Later, I would find out.

I wanted this child so much that I thought that perhaps he would change his mind. I soon found out that Eddie had this happen before with another girl and asked her to do the same. I did not know what to do. I had just started as a paraprofessional at P.S. 86 in the Bronx and did not make enough money to take care of myself. Getting thrown out of my house was going to happen. I did not know where to go or what to do.

One day, not soon after the atomic bomb dropped, Eddie and I had a date. While I was in Eddie's apartment in Brooklyn, he received a very important phone call about a very important meeting he had with office associates. *Some associates*, I thought. The conversation sounded kind of strange to me. In other words, he had to report to a boss and had to have a legitimate excuse for not making the meeting. The conversation went down something like this: "I have a situation I need to take care of. This girl is not like that. She is another type of girl, and I need to take care of this situation." Use your imagination! I had enough sense to not ask any questions or to think about it.

Does this guy have Godfather he has to report to or else? One thing Mami taught me in Spanish Harlem was, **"Tú escuchas y no hagas preguntas,"** which means "You listen and don't ask questions." In words of wisdom, she said **"El que todo lo quiere saber es porque todo lo quiere contar,"** which means "He who wants to know everything is because he wants to tell it all." And I know that I did not want to be placed into that category. What do you think happens to people like that?

Eddie took me to a very expensive clinic in Manhattan. I was put under, and then it was over. Spiritually, I felt terrible. I had committed the most horrible sin. How could I ever forgive myself? He took me to lunch at a new deli that belonged to one of his friends. They were a married couple. Guess what? It was a cover-up for a call girl service. It was so obvious! The phone rang, and it was a client. Off went the wife to take care of business. It was a real deli.

This was such a horrible experience that to this day, I cannot remember the clinic, the deli, or that couple. It is all a blur.

At home, I threw myself into Mama's arms and sobbed uncontrollably! She asked no questions but just held me. All I said in the middle of my crying was that my relationship with Eddie was a sad story. How could I even tell her? That would mean being kicked out on the street.

In the interim, I dated Eddie for about 2 years, hoping for a future with him. He was always a complete gentleman.

One evening, he seemed to be so anxious, nervous, very uneasy and had a face of guilt. He said, "I have a confession to make." It was something I did not know about him, a secret. He confessed that he was a **porn star** and told me his screen name. I thought he was making this up just to break up with me. However, I had a problem in the *Tutu Department*. This is a made-up phrase some Spanish women use to express the words for the most intimate part of their body. To say the least, I could not understand this when Eddie was the only man in my life. Of course, he denied any wrongdoings. He told me that I could have picked this up on the train or something I sat on that was unsanitary. What was he thinking? Scientifically, I knew this was impossible.

In brief, I was prescribed KWELL at the gynecologist's office. When I gave the prescription to the pharmacist, he was nervous and looked at me with great surprise. I realized this must have been something serious. Being naive is stupidity at its best! This is what I have to say about this.

Eddie later invited me to a dance place where you needed an escort to enter. It was sort of clandestine! I would say it was gloomy, murky, and almost frightening. When we entered, I saw people who were executives with dates watching people dance and swim in a pool. Some people had suits, outfits of every kind, and fancy dance dresses. Some men were members of the clergy because of what they wore. Use your imagination. Others had no clothes, and this included the clergy. I thought, *NO CLOTHES. What kind of place is this?* I did not say a word. As we toured the place, there were rooms where people were involved in the most degrading and perverted type of behavior you could possibly imagine! The first thing I thought to myself was, *THIS IS SODOM AND GOMORRAH!* This reminds me of places mentioned in the Bible. Who would ever think that a place like this really existed? I became completely disturbed and wanted out of the relationship. It was confirmed. Eddie was not making his story up.

Would you believe that I continued dating Eddie after this drama? A year later or so, he celebrated my 20th birthday at his new house. He had a custom ring made for me. There must have been at least 50 people or more at this party. I had invited my sister and her husband to the party as well as some of my colleagues. The party was great, but the events that took place after two hours or so were eye-openers. When I went into one of the bedrooms, I saw one of his friends taking pills. I thought, *is he taking drugs?* Not long after this unpleasant scene, the girls at the pool decided they were going to swim in their birthday suits. I said, "Eddie, have them put their clothes on. This is unacceptable behavior." My sister and spouse, as well as my friends, were so turned off! I was completely numb because I could not believe that Eddie would allow such behavior.

They sang happy birthday to me. What was I thinking? How could I remain at this party? I wanted so much for this man to change. Mind you, this man never, ever said an ill word to me but treated me with kindness. The insecurity of not having a normal relationship with my dad had a lot to do with it now that I think about it. I was searching for fatherly love in the wrong places. Eddie was not a **machista**, but he was in every sense of the word *PERVERTED.* I said to him one time, "You may have had other girlfriends who joined your way of life but not me. I will be the only one who does not." Would you believe that I stayed at the party when my company left? Not long after this birthday party, he wanted to date another girl. We broke up, and I suffered. I became his little therapist because his live-in girlfriend woke up every morning with a marijuana cigarette for breakfast, and she had a little girl she could not control that was overweight. To his disappointment, this so-called girlfriend of his became pregnant, and it wasn't his. It was his friend's baby, and guess who paid for another abortion? Yes, Eddie did. I said, "You want beauty and no brains. This is exactly what you wanted." Eddie was so disturbed that he uttered, "I wish I could have a combination of the two of you, beauty, and brains. If I marry you, I can make a contract that states for you to bear me three children, and I will take care of you. The only stipulation is that you do not take my house. I know you would bear intelligent children." I told him that he was sick! "Marriage is not a contract. It is a union based on love and not agreements. As matter of fact, take your money, your Cadillac Seville, your house and shove it!"

Not long after, on a strange night, Papi came home really upset. He sat my mother and me down. Papi said, "You do not know what just happened? A friend of mine went to the movies and saw Eddie on the big screen in some porno flick. You need to leave him." I was appalled because I knew that was not the way this could have happened. He was the viewer. I said, "The only way you could have known this is because you were at this porn movie yourself. He is under a completely different name. I do not believe you! This is the reason why I left him in the first place. Do not lie to me!" My Dad was not a saint. There is a saying in Spanish that goes like this, "**Tiene cola que le pisen.**" In other words, it refers to someone who does not lead a faithful life or does things that are not nice, and people know about them.

He had a tail a mile long.

About two years passed, and Eddie would not change. We still dated sporadically, but I was guarded.

Proverbs 15:22, *"Plans fail for lack of counsel, but with many advisers they succeed."*

2. The Knock on the Door

I would say that the early- to mid-'80s was the beginning of the end of the disco ERA. Ronald Reagan became president and introduced Reaganomics to reduce government regulation, the growth of government spending, and more. There also seemed to be a lot of spiritual revivals around the country. Some famous preachers were Jerry Farwell, Billy Graham, and others too numerous to list. People were searching for answers, and so was I.

It was the fall season on a bright afternoon. I can still remember wearing a pair of brown corduroy slacks with a brown-beige, long sleeve blouse. I believe I took the bus to my boyfriend's house, or he picked me up that afternoon.

I vividly remember being in his living room when some men knocked on the door. They were from Hudson View Baptist Church. They reminded Eddie about their invitation to their church. When they left, Eddie told me he was a man of his word. I said, "What do you mean a man of your word?" He said, "I told them I would stop by their church." I thought he did not believe in God. What an opportunity! I said, "Don't worry; I will go with you."

Talk about excitement. I was elated. I believe it was a Wednesday night prayer meeting. When we arrived, there were greeters at the door. Kathy, Joe, Bob and his wife, and elders of the church, just to name a few.

The sanctuary had about 10–12 pews on each side of the church where people sat and sang hymns to the Lord for about 10–15 minutes. All members had their Bibles ready to listen to the Word of God. I remember the warm welcome coming from the pews filled with parishioners. I must say that I felt so welcomed. It was a different feeling. After about 15–20 minutes, the pastor began his sermon. I don't recall what it was. I do know that it was the most engaging message. After all, it has been over 37 years since the event. However, the most paramount statements were: "If you are here today, and you believe in God but have never asked Him into your heart, you are not saved." Pastor Ron stated something like this: "You need to acknowledge that you are a sinner and make a public profession of faith before witnesses. In order to be saved, you must just simply say: Lord, I know that I am a sinner and that You died and bled on the cross for all my sins."

The book of Romans 10 verses 9, 10, 11 states the following, "That if thou shalt confess with thy mouth the Lord Jesus, and shalt believe in thine heart that God hath raised him from the dead, thou shalt be saved. For with the heart man believeth unto righteousness; and with the mouth confession is made unto salvation. For the scripture saith, for whosoever believeth in him shall not be ashamed."

When I heard this message, I had an epiphany! Oh, my goodness. I thought all along that I had to go to this church because of Eddie. When Pastor Ron invited people to come to the altar to profess their faith in Jesus, I looked at Eddie and said, "He is talking to me." I now knew that the knock on the door was not for my boyfriend that night. It was the hand of **Almighty God** that made me realize that I needed salvation. I knew about Jesus but had not ever heard about the plan of salvation. Even the demons in hell believed in Jesus but did not accept Him.

That very night, I broke up my relationship with Eddie and said, "You are not a believer, and you and I cannot continue this relationship." He was shocked and could not believe it. After all, I was deeply in love with him and hoped that he would pop the question one day. Thank God that never happened. Where would I be now? The children I gave birth to would probably never know Jesus. Praise the Lord! He created a family tree of believers right down to my entire immediate family. After this visit, I evangelized the entire family.

Matthew 13:9 states, "He who has ears, let him hear." Many people have gone to church all their lives or have been to different churches, looking for truth and trying to fill a void that only Jesus can fill. Jesus had knocked on the door of my heart for the first time.

God bless Pastor Ron for leading me to the Lord.

The day you hear that call, don't turn Him away. God says in His Word in Revelation 3:20, "Behold, I stand at the door, and knock: if any man hears my voice, and open the door, I will come into him, and will sup with him, and he with me." In other words, Jesus invites you. He knocks on the door of your heart, and you make the decision to open the door or leave it closed. Jesus gives all of us a free will. John 6:37 states, "Everyone the Father gives Me will come to Me and the one who comes to Me I will never drive away."

If you are reading this short story, it is not a coincidence. Jesus is talking to you right now. Perhaps you have been a great person all your life. You have been a good citizen, brother, sister, uncle, aunt, mother, father, friend and righteous. No one can earn salvation. If that were possible, then why did Jesus die on the cross? The book of Isaiah 64:6 states, "But we are all as an unclean thing, and all our righteousness are as filthy rags; and we all do fade as a leaf, and our iniquities, like the wind, have taken us away."

Jesus is the unblemished lamb that shed His blood for all the sins we have committed and any sin we would ever commit. John 3:16 states, "For God so loved the world that he gave his one and only Son, that whoever believes in him shall not perish but have eternal life."

Is Jesus knocking on the door of your heart? Don't delay because you never know when Jesus will call you home. Your call can be to heaven or hell.

You decide.

Acts 4:12, *"Salvation is found in no one else, for there is no other name under heaven given to mankind by which we must be saved."*

John 14:6, *"Jesus answered, 'I am the way and the truth and the life. No one comes to the Father except through me.'"*

3. What is the Price?

In the 1980s, Cats opened on Broadway; Michael Jackson released his album Thriller; and the Walkman, a cassette recorder, was popular for joggers because they could listen to music while they exercised. A spiritual revival was still going strong, and souls were being saved. There was a lot of door-to-door knocking for sharing the Good News.

At home, I shared my newfound faith. It was not received well. Mami said that I lived at this church and asked why I had to go on Sunday morning, evening, and Wednesday nights. I tried to explain, "Mami, I am not going to a discotheque or hanging out; I am just going to the house of God." I was sort of the troublemaker in the house.

Even though I paid rent, I had no say. My parents were good people who wanted us to all earn our keep, and I am all for that once you are an adult. My eldest brother would run up the phone bill, and I had to pay it. I thought that wasn't fair. I decided to get a phone installed in my room, a separate line, so that there was no confusion. Guess what happened? My eldest brother used my phone and ran up the bill, so I put a lock on it. This was a constant battle. If he did not have clean socks, he took mine because they were like his. As a last resort, I placed a lock on my bedroom door. My brother was also one of my favorites in the household because when we were children, he was my buddy, so I could not ever stay upset.

My Titi was my mentor, so I asked her for help. She spoke to my mom about this situation and said that she was going to help me get my own apartment right across the street from hers at Fort Independence in the Bronx, near Bailey Avenue.

I was so afraid! Since I was in the last semester of college, I had a lot of books. Previously, I had dropped out of college because I just needed to sort out my life. This also meant: What did I really want to do for the rest of my life? What was my passion? What were my talents?

 Although Eddie and I had broken off our relationship, he became a loyal friend. He asked a friend of his to help me move. It was free of charge, and he was not disrespectful at all. Both he and his friend moved me out on a cold winter day. I remember the cold wind and snow coming down as we tried to move as quickly as possible. The apartment was on the first floor, and I was assured that it would be safe if I had gates on the back windows facing the backyard. I purchased the gates on the window to ensure my safety. After all, my windows faced the backyard, and who would hear me if someone decided to come in? Eddie disappeared from my life but would somehow keep my friendship for about 13 years.

Unfortunately for me, I had to go to my Titi's house to sleep sometimes because the boiler in my building would break, and it was days without hot water. These freezing episodes reminded me of my cold days and nights in the Harlem ghetto apartment. Thankfully, I went to work at P.S. 86 as a paraprofessional and went directly to night school at Lehman College. It was warm as toast until the evening when I got to my apartment.
One night, I came home and found that someone had used a strong tool to pry open the gate that barred the windows facing the backyard to my apartment. "Oh, Lord," I said, "I give you 24 hours to get me out of here!" I believed it.

I spoke to my pastor, and he recommended a real estate agent. I shared my experience and how terrified I was. The pastor had recommended me. How else would I get an apartment? This was divine intervention! I moved to this lovely studio apartment with a neighborhood watch, wall-to-wall carpet, a bathroom the size of a room, a walk-in closet, a doorman who always watched, and a parking lot. I went from rags to riches!
Psalm 121: "I lift up my eyes to the mountains—where does my help come from? My help comes from the Lord, the Maker of heaven and earth. He will not let your foot slip—he who watches over you will not slumber; indeed, he who watches over Israel will neither slumber nor sleep. The Lord watches over you—the Lord is your shade at your right hand; the sun will not harm you by day, nor the moon by night. The Lord will keep you from all harm—he will watch over your life; the Lord will watch over your coming and going both now and forevermore."

Matthew 10:34–39, *"³⁴ Do not suppose that I have come to bring peace to the earth. I did not come to bring peace, but a sword. ³⁵ For I have come to turn a man against his father, a daughter against her mother, a daughter-in-law against her mother-in-law—³⁶ a man's enemies will be the members of his own household. ³⁷ Anyone who loves their father or mother more than me is not worthy of me; anyone who loves their son or daughter more than me is not worthy of me. ³⁸ Whoever does not take up their cross and follow me is not worthy of me. ³⁹ Whoever finds their life will lose it, and whoever loses their life for my sake will find it"* (also in **Luke 12:51–53).**

Chapter Six

1. Bus Ride

The '80s had some interesting events. Some were sad or informational. AT&T, for one, was obligated to break up its monopoly in January of 1984. The average price of a new car was about $8,000.00. In Monaco, Princess Grace of Monaco falls off a mountain road and dies at age 52. Her daughter Stephanie, 17, suffered serious injuries but survived. By 1983, America sent the first African, Guion Bluford, into Space.

On one of my bus rides to my parents' house in the Bronx, I met up with an old college chemistry partner, Ray, who had joined the Armed Forces. He said that he needed someone to write to. I remembered how much Ray helped me during our tutoring sessions and in chemistry class. He was handsome and was now physically fit because of boot camp.

This was the beginning of a **nightmare that would begin in Texas, continue in Germany, then end up in the Bronx.** It was a horror movie that would last for a decade or more. In Spanish, there is a saying that goes like this, **"Caras vemos pero corazones no sabemos."** In other words, we may see people's faces, but we don't know them or know anything about their hearts or intentions.

Ray had given me his address at boot camp. During training, no one was allowed any outside contact. I do not know how I did it, but I was able to get in contact with him. I was determined. Little did I know that any door that is hard to open should not be opened. This was not God's will. When he finished training, we started dating. He immediately asked me to marry him. My mom met him but did not see him enough times to be able to evaluate him as a mate for me. He took me to his house to meet his family during the Christmas Holiday. Immediately, his mother thought I was Dominican. That was a compliment for me, but for them, it was not. They had a very deep-rooted Spanish background and did not appreciate the color of my skin or the texture of my hair, if you know what I mean. Nevertheless, they were very welcoming and very generous people.

My pastor was not pleased with this relationship and asked members of my congregation not to throw me a bridal shower. This was hearsay, but their behavior seemed to indicate that. A member and his wife invited me to their apartment and gave me their blessing. I wish the pastor would have approached me and had a very serious talk with me. However, he had preached about this topic, so I had no excuse. I was an adult and should have sought his counsel. Since I was a new babe in the Lord, I didn't really realize how serious or detrimental it was to be unequally yoked.

I still was determined to marry, so Mom paid for my wedding dress, and I went to a dressmaker who was able to make it on short notice.
Since I worked in a school, I informed my principal about getting married and living in another state so that he could hire another teacher.

My fiancé rented a furnished apartment a walking distance from Fort Sam Houston base in San Antonio, Texas. There was a Baptist church down the block that we attended, and I was very happy about this. We went to the justice of the peace and got married. One of Ray's Army buddies and his girlfriend were the witnesses. Our weekend honeymoon was in Nuevo Laredo, Texas, where we were able to experience Mexican culture.

All was well; however, one night, when I sat on Ray's lap and looked into his eyes, I saw something I could not understand. It was kind of strange, and I shared this feeling I had about him. I said, "You seem to be hiding something, and I do not know what it is." He was not happy about it. He changed the subject, and we did not speak about it again. It was sort of my intuition or something. You know, sometimes, we have this gut feeling about something or someone, and we dismiss it. DON'T DO IT! YOU WILL BE SORRY!

Ray was so helpful around the apartment the first few months of our marriage. I guess you can call this the honeymoon stage. There were times we lay on the grass and looked up at the stars. We also went to Tex-Mexican dancing with his Army buddies, or they came to visit us.

Ray liked to drink with his friends and have them over. Unfortunately, I later found out that two of his friends who came to visit us with their girlfriends were living in adultery, and their wives were away until they sent for them. Mami always said, **"Dime con quién andas y te diré quien eres,"** which means "Birds of a feather flock together."

Since Ray finished medical training at Fort Sam, San Antonio, I had to return to New York City to live with his parents and grandmother because Ray had to fill out paperwork before I could join him in Wiesbaden, Germany. I wrote him a letter every single day. I was really in love.

His grandmother made it her business to get me a job in Co-op City right on the first floor of their building as a doctor's assistant with cardiologists during the months of June, July, and August. All I had to do was take the elevator down and go straight to the office. I would come upstairs to eat lunch. One day, his grandmother locked me out so that I would not be able to eat lunch. Would you believe she was sitting right at home? I told my mother-in-law, and she had a talk with her. Apparently, she had given her trouble all her married life to her son because they always lived together. Grandma ruled the roost.

By the end of the summer, I flew to Wiesbaden, Germany. Ray had an apartment in a German community like ten blocks away or so from the American Army-Air Force Hospital Base. Our neighbors were from Spain and took a liking to my husband but grew to love me. I was not alone. I quickly bonded with Army-Air Force members and joined a local non-denominational church. Ray went with me and was very helpful. I said, "Perhaps I can join the Armed Forces while I am here. This will boost our income." Ray raised his voice a couple of decibels and said, "Oh no, you are not going to pull rank on me. You have a degree, and you are a teacher. This means you'll be an officer, and I'm not having it." I was devastated! I thought we would benefit with one of us as an officer. Oh no, I had married a male chauvinist swine! I left one from my immediate family and found one in my own husband overseas.

I placed fifty-one applications before I landed a job. Most of the jobs I applied for were for teaching assignments. The first place of employment was with teaching Armed Force men who had not earned a diploma. By then, I was carrying Angela, and Ray wanted me to get an abortion, but I would not do it. He wanted us to wait 8 years, but by then, I would be 32 years of age. Throughout my entire pregnancy, he was not loving at all. One night, while I sat on the sofa, he grabbed Angela's leg or arm while in utero. I said, "Are you out of your mind?" I cried a whole lot. One day, I had a craving for Chinese soup, and he yelled at me from the top of his lungs, saying, "I am not going to go crazy satisfying your urges." A pre-eclampsia condition set in. I swelled up, and Angela was born 3 weeks before her due date. I was in danger and did not realize it. My hospital stay was almost two weeks. I had a nurse at my bedside almost 24/7. Wiesbaden Air Force Medical is an excellent facility with high vigilance. I was not allowed to shower alone or go to the bathroom unless escorted.

At first, it didn't matter because my insides were so swollen. I couldn't release my own body fluids; I needed a catheter. I said, "Oh, this is great. I was almost aborted before I was born, then taken to the emergency room a couple of months after I was born because of my hyperactivity, and now I could almost die. Oh, God, what could this all mean?"

Members of the armed forces, at the drug testing lab, who worked with Ray, really liked us, and gave me a huge baby shower right at the lab. Then the members of our local church did the same. It was like having a big family. I can say I had everything I needed.

In the winter of 1984, it was extremely cold in Germany. It was a cold chill that just wormed itself right into your bones. Ray refused to increase the heat. We were warm while we slept, but Angela started to cry, and Ray said, "She'll calm down." My mother's common sense told me something was wrong. I could still remember that night. I picked Angela up, and she was so cold that I took her in my arms and did not allow her to sleep in her crib until she was able to walk months later. What a terrible feeling! My baby could have frozen to death had I not paid attention to her cry. Even though she had very warm pajamas, mittens so that she would not scratch her face, a baby night hat, and warm blankets, she was not warm enough. You can only imagine what color she was turning. Later in life, Angela would do something very special that would make a difference in people's quality of life. **There is a purpose for every single being under the sun.**

When the baby and I were home, Ray's mom, Mina, flew in from New York City and stayed for about two weeks. She wanted to see our baby so badly and was blown away by her beauty. Later, she would be my ally.

Right after six weeks, I returned to work and had this wonderful officer's wife babysit Angela until I was recommended to the Army-Airforce nursery right next to Ray's laboratory. He was able to walk right next door to check up on our baby. She had an olive complexion with blue eyes until she was about 8 months old when they turned hazel green. I got a phone call every single day at work. They said, "She refuses to drink her milk or eat and cries a lot. She's gorgeous, but she is awful!"

Two of the caretakers fell in love with Angela. She was a beautiful baby. It was these two women who helped Angela transition into nursery daycare, which, by the way, was top-notch. Everyone stopped me on the bus or the street. On Sundays, a German lady carried Angela during the entire church service. She was the mother of 5 boys and longed for a daughter.

By this time, I was accepted as a second-grade teacher in Mainz Elementary School. A member of my women's prayer group, Kathy Hinton, recommended me. Unbeknownst to me, I was carrying my second child and had a menstrual period for two months. In my case, Spanish women from prior centuries say it is called **luna llena,** a full moon—when you're on the rag as regularly scheduled, and fertilization still occurs. The only reason I became suspicious was that this little boy in my second-grade class who hugged me every single day said, "You feel heavier today around the waist." On top of that, the smell of popcorn turned my stomach. My second-grade class regularly had popcorn with me on Fridays. I made it in the classroom the old fashion style.

Ray was determined to leave the service by September of 1985. My goal was to save as much money as possible to buy property when we returned to the United States. This went on for 18 months while in Germany. However, I thought we would stay longer. I could not understand why Ray did not want to make this his career. He was a field medic and worked in what was called the PEE LAB. This was a lab that the armed forces used to test soldiers for drugs unannounced. This meant that at any given time, members of the armed forces came in and watched while soldiers gave their urine samples for drug testing.

Mami kept in contact and said she would babysit for me if I returned to the United States. This was a temptation for me because I was homesick but loved life in Germany. I had grown accustomed to the food, the local church, the weather, and the people. Basically, I did not want to return. However, she assured me she would babysit.

Sometimes I wondered if drugs were the reason Ray wanted to leave. After all, he did not exhibit any signs of addiction, except for German beer. However, there were several peculiar incidents I found very disturbing. On 3 to 4 occasions, he lost my paycheck. His excuse was that it was windy and freezing cold when he had to pull out his wallet at the base's check-in gate, and somehow, my money was lost. It is so funny now that I think about it because it was always my money that fell out of a hole in his pocket and accidentally got lost.

There is only one statement for this state of mine at the time, *"No hay mas ciego que el que no quiere ver."* This literally means that there is no one more blind than one who does not want to see reality. You are just delusional!

Over time, Ray became extremely volatile, and I could not make any comments about any of my opinions, and the music on the weekends was unbearable. Our Spanish next-door neighbors started to really dislike Ray when they asked him to turn down the music one night. They told him he had no right to wear the crucifix he was wearing because he wasn't worthy of wearing one.

On September 16, 1985, Genevieve was born. Ray seemed very nervous because he thought something would be wrong with the baby. I did not think anything of it because I had pneumonia and feared something could go wrong because I was so ill, but she was perfect. Ray was allowed in the delivery room because he wanted to make sure that Genevieve had all her extremities. Go figure that one out. By November 6, 1985, I would leave Germany for the United States, and Ray would now be a civilian. We would have to start all over. In the meantime, I would have to travel alone with our girls.

Lufthansa must be the best airline. Since I was traveling alone with a toddler and an infant, one of Lufthansa's airline stewardesses drove me to one of their offices in an airport car and offered me breakfast. When it was time to board the plane, I was driven to the front of the line. During the entire plane ride, airline attendants helped me with both children. Upon arrival, my family had gathered to welcome me home at the airport, and so did Ray's parents. They did not recognize me because I had gained so much weight.

Proverbs 15:22, *"Plans fail for lack of counsel, but with many advisers they succeed."*

2. The Secret is Out!

During the 1980s, AIDS and HIV affected many people, and doctors did not know what to do to find a cure. This disease was a concern for the entire world. I was so worried about it that I had Angela's and Genevieve's ears pierced in Germany before taking them to the United States.

Living abroad was very exciting; however, I felt as if my native country, The Great United States of America, was calling for my return. I considered myself a real patriot.

Since my husband decided to leave the United States Army from Wiesbaden, Germany, we had to leave the country.

In November of 1985, I had to return to New York City from Germany. I had the privilege of working as a teacher in Mainz, Kastel, for the Army and Airforce. It was very early in my teaching career. Somehow, I felt that I still needed to venture out and try other careers.

I had to return to the United States with our girls alone. Ray said that I needed to go ahead while he left everything in order before being honorably discharged from the Army.

At the time, we had no place to live, so we moved in with my in-laws in Co-op City located in the Bronx. This meant that we would have to live a couple of months with Ray's extended family until we both obtained employment. Ray's grandmother still resided in the same co-op apartment. She was by far the most difficult member of this extended family. His parents were the most generous human beings on planet Earth!

It was a very difficult time for me with one toddler and one infant. After all, I still was not well enough to work. I was getting over pneumonia and trying to gain full strength.

After two or three weeks, Ray arrived with an honorable discharge from the Army to New York City. Our girls were about eighteen months and about three months old. Ray's parents gave us their master bedroom in Co-op City.

Ray began searching for employment, and so did I. I wanted to spread my wings to try another profession and not return to elementary school teaching. I must have been too anxious to start work. I had pneumonia, and my back was out of whack! My physician in Germany recommended and encouraged me to stay home for a couple of weeks after I had Genevieve.

At night, Ray exhibited erratic behavior. One evening, Ray's mother said to him, "Ray, you look so pale!" I began to feel helpless and hopeless. It could have been hormonal since I still was postpartum.

Since Ray's behavior was so unpredictable, I asked him to show me our bank account. To my surprise, close to all $10,000 had disappeared from our savings account. It was so upsetting that I still do not even remember what excuse he gave me. Between his lies, no place of our own, and my postpartum condition, I felt physically very weak. Even though I was a fighter, I refused to accept that I just was too weak to make a rash decision. You see, I had saved this amount of money in Germany by depositing my entire check every two weeks. I was very frugal and made sure that everything I needed was obtained by word of mouth at my local church. Members of my congregation had a system of getting second-hand bassinets, change tables, cribs, carriages, and infant clothing. Everything I did was on a budget. We were even able to go on vacation to Spain and Africa while overseas because of a planned vacation on a budget.

In the middle of all this mishmash, I thought, *where are we going to go? I can't go to my parents' house because they wouldn't even take me in.*

Ray found a job as an AVIS driver, so some money was coming in. However, he did not last long. By now, I was employed at the Bronx Supreme Court on 161 Street and Grand Concourse as a Spanish Interpreter. My mother-in-law's neighbor gave me an opportunity, and it was a great fit. It was on a per-diem basis. I trained well for one month. Money was very reasonable. However, this job was temporary, and per-diem interpreters always had delayed payments. Eventually, I had to leave to find another job.

One day, I just woke up and told my mother-in-law, Mina, "I am going to start packing my things and start looking for an apartment." She said, "Elsie, where are you going? How can you talk about moving out if you don't have any money?" My response was, "I believe what I am saying to be true. All I must do is believe that My Lord will provide."

Thank goodness that there was some money left to try to rent an apartment of our own. I had a maternal aunt who was my mentor for most of my life. She put in a word with the superintendent of her building on 2857 Sedgwick Avenue for apartment 5C. I was able to rent a beautiful two-bedroom apartment on the fifth floor. The apartment building had a very large vestibule. It also had two sections in the building with two elevators. My apartment faced the front of the building with breathtaking sites of the reservoir and a beautiful skyline.

The apartment was right across from Our Lady of Angels Church, and there was a bus stop right in front. There was also another bus stop in the opposite direction in front of a C-Town Supermarket down the block with a laundromat next door, a middle school two blocks down, and a huge park across the street. The park had towering trees over it, and behind the park benches was a tall wall.

Every morning, the sun shone through the front windows, but in the summer, it was so hot. It did not matter to me because I considered it our space. The rent was about $550.00 a month.

Meanwhile, Ray would disappear with friends. I never thought anything about it. When he returned home, he looked as pale as a ghost. I knew something was up but was not able to pinpoint what it was. He was helpful with the kids and was searching for employment. Finally, Ray did find a job with The New York City Health Department to ensure young children were lead-free.

One morning, I discovered some kind announcement in the local paper or television about some trailers found in some locations of the city to help people seek employment for free. All you had to do was share your qualifications and the salary you wanted to earn. If possible, they would try to find employment to match your profile along with the income you desired.

I found a job at Global Business Institute on 125th Street. My job was to teach an English class to adults who sought higher education. I loved it! Meanwhile, I needed a babysitter. My mother-in-law was still working at the factory as a sample maker and could not take care of my children. While in Germany, my mother assured me that she would babysit if I returned to the United States. When I inquired about it, she stated that she could not because she had to work. However, she said my sister would babysit. This was not in my sister's plans. Mom had volunteered my sister. She did not want to let me down because she knew how desperate I was. It was too much at the time because she had three children, and my two made it five toddlers. Basically, it was practically a nursery. However, she did care for our girls for a while. God bless her!

While Ray and I were in Germany, we used to discuss savings, purchases, and entertainment. Now, having a conversation about paying bills was turning into a problem.

One night, I wanted to look at the finances, and Ray became very violent! He backed me into our bedroom. There was a window with no way out. I was so afraid that I thought perhaps he would suffocate me. I thought to myself, for some odd reason, *what would a character on a comedy show do to escape a room?* How ironic that I would think of such a thing! Sometimes, television with a lot of humor gives you great ideas on how to think on your feet when you're in a bind.

I thought to myself, *scope the room for the closest object you could use just to make it out of the room.* This is exactly what I did. I grabbed a lamp that was on the left side of my dresser and broke it on Ray's head—just enough to escape from the room. I then said, "My father used to hit me, and you are not my father. I will pay the man who thinks he is going to put his hands on me!"

When the lamp hit his head, he came out of the trance, wept like a child, and apologized. Ray jumped into a hot tub to gather his thoughts while he sat in shock. The girls were sleeping because this incident occurred during the evening hours. Thank God!

I sat on my bed in shock, disappointed, confused, and lost for words. Somehow, my inner voice said, "What you are looking for is in his wallet." I thought, *this doesn't make sense. How can the answer be in his wallet?* I had never looked through my husband's personal belongings because I trusted him. Now, I wanted to rule out my suspicion. I looked around the room for Ray's pants since he was still sitting in a hot tub. When I found his pants, my heart started to race fast, and I started to feel terror at the thought of finding out a horrible truth. Frantically, I looked through every pocket and found his black wallet with his license and, oh, wait, another card. The card had the words 'Methadone Clinic Photo I.D. Outpatient on it.

The frustration, deception, and helplessness hit me in the face, and these feelings propelled me right into the bathroom. "You're a drug addict! Therefore, all our money has dried up, and we're broke! I am calling your mother and father right now!"

My in-laws must have driven one hundred miles an hour from Co-op City to 2857 Sedgwick Avenue. They arrived in just twenty minutes. They rang the bell and then knocked on our door. I blurted out, "Ray is a drug addict, and here's the proof."

Mina, Ray's mother, then confessed that she had been paying our $550.00 a month for rent. I told her, "How could you bail him out? You can't continue to pay, and I can't do it alone."

Now, I understand why Ray kept getting parking tickets. He probably left his car anywhere just to get a fix. This was scary, irresponsible, and unacceptable. What could I do?

Anyway, I had to come up with a plan and do it fast! We didn't owe any money for rent and didn't want to start that. After all, Auntie was the person who had recommended us for this apartment, and I did not want to embarrass her.

Ray told his parents that he wanted to come clean. He said "I would go through COLD TURKEY" if we moved back to his parents in Co-op City again.

I thought to myself, *here we go again!* Moving was a hassle with two children. I packed for days. My poor father-in-law and brother-in-law helped us move. My father-in-law also had a friend who gave us an inexpensive storage space at his house.

Although Auntie already found out the news, she watched how fast we moved out. She said, "You look like a bunch of gypsies moving out in the middle of the night, even though it was early in the evening." I had such a heavy heart. The only friend I had was God, and that was all I needed. I wondered what I could learn from all this. Little did I know that I still had a lot to learn. How much must a wife have to tolerate her husband's physical, emotional, and financial abuse for asking questions about household matters?

I found consolation in the Word of God and in the council of others at my local church. We settled into Co-op City again, into Ray's parents' master bedroom.

My morning began at 4:00 a.m. because I had to cook dinner, prepare my children's breakfast and lunch for their sitter located on Kingsbridge Road. She was a member of my local church. I had to take two buses with two toddlers.

Despite everything, there were three generations living together in this apartment. Ray's grandmother had the habit of making my life and Mina's life miserable. She basically ran the show.

Although Ray had a car, he slept through it all until his mom told me, "Get him up. You should not have to get on buses when he could drop you off." I didn't feel comfortable even mentioning this because I wanted to avoid conflicts at all costs.

Ray reluctantly got up in the morning to help me because I was fed up with him sleeping in until he had to go to work. My argument was, "Why should you be the only one benefiting from the car when we both work?"

At night, when we arrived home, I had to face a messy kitchen because Grandma had cooked, left a mess, and told the rest of the family that I had left the kitchen a disaster in the morning. They knew better than this because Mina got ready for work while I had already finished in the kitchen and had cleaned up. It was so frustrating because every morning, I cleaned the kitchen so that members of the family would find it clean.

During the evening hours, Ray was helpful. After I fed and bathed the girls, he put them to bed while I had a cup of coffee alone in the kitchen to wind down. Mina would come into the kitchen to ask me what I was doing, having a cup of coffee, while her son was putting the girls to bed alone. I understood this was a cultural thing, and it was so difficult.

I prayed every night. Sometimes, it was midnight when I opened my Bible and kneeled in the bathroom because it was the only place I was not disturbed. Grandma would say, "You should never open a Bible at midnight; that's bad luck." She had beliefs that I didn't even want to talk about because all I wanted was quiet time with my Lord to pray.

Ray's parents were so generous and so loving that they could not see past their son's shortcomings. He went COLD TURKEY and had the entire family's support. It was terrible to watch. He finally was clean for a couple of months. We had no money because we had to pay the credit card bills and parking tickets again. As a result, I opened a bank account.

Springtime was around the corner, and I started packing up my winter clothes and other items. Mina saw me packing and said, "What are you doing?" I said, "I'm moving." She said, "How can you move if you have no money?" My response was that I believed I would and had no doubt. My mom spoke to the superintendent in her building for a one-bedroom, ground-floor apartment located on 2609 Aqueduct Avenue in the Bronx on Kingsbridge Road.

Mina was surprised but happy. I had so much faith that I did move out. Mina said, "Elsie, you have so much faith that you were already packed without even having a place."

Life seemed to smile at us. Ray got a job for the MTA buses in NYC Transit. Now, our babysitter was about five blocks down. I had a twin carriage to take my girls to the same babysitter on Kingsbridge Road and Sedgwick Avenue.

1 Peter 5:7, *"Cast all your anxiety on him because he cares for you."*

Chapter Seven

1. Prayer Vigil

In the late '80s and early '90s, there were popular Christian songs. Some of the top hits were: "Heaven" by BeBe & CeCe Winans and "Forever Friends" by Sandi Patti.

Sometimes, in life, we need some major breakthroughs, especially if you have a loved one on substance abuse, who has disappeared from the face of the earth. What do you do?

I was already a single parent with two girls ages 4 and 5 in a ground floor apartment on 2609 Aqueduct Avenue in the Bronx. My husband was addicted to cocaine, methadone, or both, as far as I knew. Fortunately, I discovered his addiction one evening when my children, who were toddlers at the time, were asleep. This incident happened in our Sedgwick Avenue apartment, across from Our Lady of Angels Church that my aunt helped me to find when I returned from Wiesbaden, Germany.

Going back about two years or so, my so-called in-laws told me about a situation. What I did not know was that Ray's parents were paying our rent. This meant that my husband was using all the funds to support his habit. I could not understand why his parents had not said anything. However, they did express how puzzled they were because our earnings were approximately **$50,000 a year.** Had they said something to me, perhaps I would have discovered his habit faster. When I started to piece previous events from Germany all the way to the United States, I understood why my husband may have wanted to get out of the Army. To top it off, he had a habit of returning home late and looking pale as a ghost when we were already living in his parents' Co-op City apartment. This had to be the drugs! It was so noticeable that his mother mentioned it one evening. This also explains how almost the entire savings we had accrued overseas in Wiesbaden, Germany, were almost liquidated!

After a heated argument with my in-laws, I said that at that moment, we did not owe any rent, and I wanted to make sure that we left the apartment before owing a dime. After all, Auntie had put in a good word for us, and I did not want my aunt to lose her integrity, and I certainly did not want to lose mine either.

What my aunt did not know was that her nephew-in-law was on drugs. I felt too embarrassed to share this sad story. My own family did not know. Another huge reason was that I did not want my two cousins who lived in the same building to find out. They would have told him off. When they were through, my brothers would probably find out and give him a piece of their minds.

I wanted to avoid this type of drama. This was a terrible and scary episode that I later would share with my immediate family.

What followed the drama from the Sedgwick Avenue apartment and Co-op City was the beginning of another nightmare on Aqueduct Avenue. By then, I had left a job at a business school and an interpreter's job at the Bronx Supreme Court. I was now working at P.S. 86 in the Bronx because when I was still living in Co-op City, a former colleague at P.S. 86X had said to me at the bus stop on Kingsbridge Road, "You should return; I am sure the administration will hire you again."

Now, fast forward a year and some months, Ray was clean for a couple of months, and now the family began being short of money again. Money began missing from the apartment because, no matter where I hid it, he would always find it. This also included a Kotex box where I hid the Lord's tithes. I thought, *surely, he would not dare to touch God's money.*

As previously mentioned, I had returned to the NYC school system as a teacher. We still lived on Aqueduct Avenue in the Bronx, where I rented an apartment in the same building as my mother.

One morning, Rene demanded money for lunch, and there was only about five to ten dollars in cash in the house that was accounted for. It was his habit to always get his way. This time, I was not going to bend or submit. He became violent, and I had to defend myself. I did not know what to do because our girls were up in their bedroom, and they had never witnessed an act of violence. I had to grab a kitchen pot full of cold water and hit him over the head.

Unfortunately, our girls saw this cat-and-dog fight, and I knew that he had to leave for good. I did not want our girls to believe that this was a way of life. Ray asked me to call the ambulance because he was bleeding and about to pass out. I said, "No. I am the victim, and I am not about to allow you to become the victim when you are the abuser!" That was when Ray confessed that he had been pretending that he was going to work. I said, "Then what on earth were you doing every single day when you put on your uniform for the MTA?" Guess what? He spilled the beans and told me that he had an accident, and they discovered he was on drugs.

When our daughters went upstairs to Abuela's house, guess what they said to Abuela? "Grandma, Mommy beat Daddy up." This is it! I had to do a lot of explaining.

Now, I needed a plan to get my husband's keys without telling him he could never come back. I allowed him back for one night, and when he fell asleep, I took the keys until I could change the lock. I was so afraid that after I took his keys, I bolted the door and set up an alarm system. He was furious, and so were his parents.

Finally, he was out, and I informed his parents that I was sending back the package. That package was him. Even though I threw him out, I still loved him and did not believe in divorce. I thought to myself, *I cannot raise my kids in such a dangerous situation, be left out in the street because of a man. My girls would begin to think this is a normal way of life.* I am not about to continue a vicious cycle. My father was an alcoholic and had volatile outbursts, and now I see this in my spouse. To add icing to the cake, my father-in-law was also an alcoholic and, on occasion, put his hands on my mother-in-law until she let him have it one day. She told me this herself.

Ray was then M.I.A. Where on earth was he? Not too long after, Ray seemed to have disappeared from the face of the earth. I thought I could pray with a friend who had a very similar situation.

One day, one of my sisters from the church, who had the same situation, decided to hold an overnight vigil to pray for our spouses who were still in bondage to drugs. We were both separated from our significant others. My friend had one daughter, and I had two. We decided to hold the vigil at her house because she had more room for three girls.

During the entire night, we prayed for our husbands' salvation and to be free of drugs. I specifically prayed that God would wake up Ray wherever he was knocked out from drugs. I also asked that God give him the strength to come home. When I say home, I mean his parents' home.

After the night vigil, I expected something because I believed our prayers would be answered.

So far, Ray had missed our youngest daughter's kindergarten graduation, even though I hoped that he would miraculously show up. His parents attended, and so did my closest friends and Mom.

In the meantime, I kept in contact with his parents. They feared that he was dead somewhere because he was missing for more than a month. All they would say was, "Where could he be?"

One day, I received a phone call from my mother-in-law. She said, "Come to Co-op City. Ray just called and told his father to hurry to a place at a park and to pick him up, or they will kill him."

I had no idea who would possibly want my husband dead if he had no enemies. Somehow, deep inside, I knew in my heart that Ray had to have done something. Why else would someone be after you?

After the dust settled, Ray confessed that he got involved with selling drugs, and instead of turning in the money, he took the money and used some of the drugs for himself that he was supposed to be selling.

Ray was hiding from these people because he feared for his life. Going back to the drama, during his phone call, he told his father to be prompt, or he'd be dead as a doornail. His father found the location and drove around with his car. He spotted his son, and Ray was able to get into his father's car in the nick of time before being spotted by these people who found themselves in the same vicinity. As a matter of fact, they missed Ray by a matter of seconds, or these drug dealers would have caught him. This would have made the news, that's for sure.

After the news, I went to my in-laws' house to see how I could help. Ray needed a bath and was unrecognizable! My heart broke with compassion for him.

When the family and I got him cleaned up and made him comfortable, he shared his story. Ray said that he passed out in some park, and that suddenly, he woke up and didn't know where he was. That was when he decided to call his father. The funny thing was that at that very hour, I prayed for him to wake up, and he woke up.

Faith moves mountains. You will never know how powerful prayer can be if you give up. Not long after, my in-laws decided to move out of state to save their son, Ray. My daughters and I went to see them off and to give them our blessing.

What Ray did not know was that I was also praying that he would not be in our lives. This prayer was answered also because I prayed for him to be out of the state, where he resides to this very day with a great job in a hospital. Tough love saved his life and led to a professional career.

Prayer is the answer when there is nothing else you can do. As a matter of fact, prayer should be the first thing that you do.

Matthew 18:20, *"For where two or three are gathered together in my name, there am I in the midst of them."*

2. Wurlitzer Piano

There were numerous popular songs like "Girl You Know It's True" by Milli Vanilli and "Straight Up" by Paul Abdul.

When Angela and Genevieve were about four and five years of age, I needed to make sure they had extracurricular activities that helped them develop their primary reading and writing skills. They weren't readers yet, so what could I do? I read this magazine article about how music helps children with basic skills that include reading from left to right and math.

When I used to work as a bilingual teacher's assistant, a teacher told me about her granddaughter who played the piano like an angel. She recommended Miss Mabel Gerber in the Bainbridge area of the Bronx to everyone. Miss Gerber had a reasonable price for piano lessons. I wanted the same for my girls but wondered about what my colleague thought was a reasonable price for piano lessons. Anyway, I decided to take a risk and go to this piano studio to see what Miss Gerber had to offer.

On a Saturday morning, I went to the address my colleague gave me. There was a delicatessen across the street, a supermarket, a bus stop on the corner, and a train station. The piano studio was in an apartment building on the first floor facing the front, with a window shade open. You could see Miss Gerber teaching a piano lesson to a student. At the entrance of the building, there were three steps that led you to a mini courtyard about fifty or more steps before you got to the first double doors. When I walked through the first double doors of the entrance, I had to walk up 5–7 steps before reaching the second double doors to ring a buzzard with Miss Gerber's name. When I rang the bell, Miss Gerber opened, and I stated that my colleague had recommended her, so she invited us in. The studio was kind of gloomy. There was a bathroom on your left when you came in, a waiting room to your right for students waiting their turn for a lesson, and a living room you could see from the street. The student who was at the piano was waiting patiently while Miss Gerber gave me the run-down. "Your five-year-old can begin for $5.00, and your four-year-old can join my rhythm band for $3.00." I sat in the studio for about an hour to watch a couple of lessons. For one, Miss Gerber was very passionate about music, and it was evident in the way she taught a lesson. There was a prescribed book for each student based on what they had learned. The conversation went down like this: "Play your scales," and of course, Miss Gerber had separate conversations in the middle of it all.

If there was an error playing the scales, she stopped in mid-sentence and took care of business. This meant she modeled how the student should position their hands and fingering across the piano keys; they had to sound evenly connected without choppiness. She continued to still talk to parents for the next part of the lesson by asking the student to pull out the pieces they had the week before. She would listen, prescribe their next steps, and assign another piece.

However, she would have the student try to play the new piece on their own to see how well they knew their music. In other words, if you were playing your previous pieces by memory and did not look at the score sheet, it was evident in the following pieces. Parents did not have to go to any music store to pick up the prescribed pieces for a new book. Ms. Gerber purchased what she knew her clientele needed at a reduced price. This meant you got a discount too! She thought of everything. Miss Gerber wanted to make sure each student would be ready for their next level of piano playing.

I tell you; this music teacher was not made a piano teacher; she was born a piano teacher. What passion! Her lesson was about 35 minutes or more because she loved to talk to parents who waited for their child's lesson. On Saturday, around 11:00 a.m., Miss Gerber scheduled her rhythm band practice for 4-year-olds in front of her piano. Some of the rhythm instruments I remember were triangles, cymbals, xylophones, shakers, maracas, bells, tambourines, and more. She played an accompanying piece the students had to follow and signaled the next steps. Attention was paid to how each instrument was held and played. Miss Gerber had enthusiasm and charisma that was transmitted to her students. There was counting, eye contact, nodding, and children marching. Children marched in a circle, playing their rhythm instruments. It was fun.

Miss Gerber cared about all her students. It didn't matter who you were or your economic status. In her eyes, you had the right to have the same opportunities to learn about music, even though you didn't have enough to pay for a lesson. Therefore, I only paid $5.00 for my five-year-old and only $3.00 for my four-year-old. Her recitals were held at P.S. 8. It was an opportunity for students to perform for a real live audience.

As weeks and seasons passed, our trip to the piano studio went from 1 day to 2 days. While I waited for my girls' turn, I helped students in the waiting room with their homework. This made time, in my mind, zoom or fly by quickly.

For practice at home, we had an electric keyboard. It was good enough for practice until my girls started playing more advanced pieces, and the mini-electric piano did not have all the keys found on a regular piano. What could I do? I couldn't buy a piano; there was no money in my budget for that. I did what I did well, and that was pray, pray, and pray for a miracle and **THINK BIG!** My prayer was very specific.

I prayed for a piano to walk through my door. Not literally a walk, but that was how I had envisioned it. I shared this specific prayer request with one of my colleagues at my school, who happened to be part of a team of teachers I worked closely with. She laughed or was very amused by it and said, "A piano coming through your door sounds impossible." I said, "Nothing is impossible. If we have the faith the size of a mustard seed, it's all it takes for your smallest of dreams to come true."

Throughout a month, I was on my knees, imploring God for a piano. The prayer went something like this. "Dear Lord, my little girls need a piano, and only You can provide me with one for them. You can create miracles. You say that anything that we ask for in Your name, You will provide. If we don't ask, we don't receive. I believe You can do anything. No one believes me." I made a request at the piano studio by expressing my needs. Faith and work go together. "God, please, grant me this petition. It is not for me; it's for my little girls." God only knows what else I said.

One day, after one month or so of prayer, I went to the piano studio, as usual, still expecting this miracle. Miss Gerber knew about our need for a piano. While she was giving a lesson to one of her clients, she shared his need to rid himself of an old-fashioned upright Wurlitzer piano to make room for the new one his parents had purchased. They were looking to give

ELSIE MADRID - MARTINEZ

it away. I said I would take it but had no way of getting it to my apartment. The boy's mother said that for $50.00, they would deliver the piano to my first-floor apartment.

That following Saturday, my doorbell rang, and in came the piano through my front door. I couldn't wait to share this blessing with my colleague, the miracle I prayed for. Long story short, she could not believe it. She said she would never doubt what came out of my mouth because I believed what I said and had no doubt.

Matthew 21:22, *"If you believe, you will receive whatever you ask for in prayer."*

3. The Man Across the Street

Two important events were publicized around the world when I was attending City College. Nelson Mandela was freed from prison and became a leader. East and West Germany were reunited after the tearing down of the Soviet Union Wall.

One spring evening, I had to attend my master's program at City College for teachers. It was my last semester. My mother, Gloria Esther, was going to move permanently to Colombia, South America, to join my father, Nestor, who was already retired. Mom said that I had to finish this master's program in eighteen months, and I thought it was very reasonable because Mom had committed herself to taking care of Angela and Genevieve after school. However, a neighbor who lived on the second floor would meet a Riverdale Pre-school bus in front of my building for my youngest daughter Genevieve and would hold Angela from 3:15 p.m. until my mother picked them up around 4:00 p.m.

By now, I was already a single parent and was so appreciative that not only did I have a wonderful mother, but I also had a great neighbor who pitched in from the goodness of her heart to make sure I made my 4:00 p.m. class. After all, both my neighbor and Mom had a full-time job and were probably tired after a full day's work. I, of course, left my daughters a full course meal every time I had class. Mom, on the other hand, provided dinner on Fridays.

Anyway, one night, after class, there was a lot of traffic. Sometimes I lost my way home because I was really exhausted and would miss a turn or an exit. My days began at 4:30 a.m. because I had to prepare meals for the day and get ready for work before my daughters woke up. When I was not at school, I was taking the girls to piano lessons, doing homework with them, completing night school assignments, or sewing new dresses for them.

One evening, I arrived home very late due to traffic and weariness. This meant that I would get home after 10:00 p.m. or later from City College night classes. I would have to look for parking and run home as quickly as possible. It was kind of scary around Kingsbridge Road in the evening hours. Cars were being broken into among other incidents that had happened in the neighborhood.

Late on the evening in question, I was fortunate enough to find a parking spot directly across the street from my apartment building. I was so happy because this meant not walking down a deserted street. As I exited my car, I saw an unfamiliar face in front of my apartment building who seemed to be ringing buzzards. I could not see which buzzards he was pressing because I was across the street. Suddenly, I heard an inner voice that said, "Watch that guy; he looks like he's up to no good." I thought to myself, *What a ridiculous thought!* However, my intuition told me differently. It might sound kind of crazy, but I preferred being crazy for a minute than to feel very sorry.

Nevertheless, I crossed the street and found myself next to the man who was ringing buzzards but stopped when he saw me approach the building. I was calm and collected but terrified inside. I was determined not to open the door with my key. I thought this would keep me safe, but I prayed, "Oh, Lord, let some people come into the building because I have no intention of opening the door to the entrance, and I definitely am not taking out my keys." Suddenly, this young man asked me nicely to ring my bell, sort of hinting that he was giving me the opportunity to ring a buzzard bell, but I said, "No, you can ring the buzzard." When the man rang a buzzard, guess whose buzzard it was? It was my bell. I quickly thought on my feet and told the young man, "I guess no one is home, but there is a store on the corner where you can make a phone call." The man agreed to go to the store down the block, and then, at the blink of an eye, people arrived in front of my building with a van to deliver a refrigerator to some apartment. I ran in and closed my apartment door on the first floor. I knew that I was in the palm of Almighty God's hand!

That night, I was sure that God had sent an angel to whisper in my heart that I was in imminent danger. I learned that night **Psalm 91:11, *"For he will order his angels to protect you wherever you go."*** *Never ignore the voice of God in your inner soul.*

4. Christmas Tree Miracle

In the Christmas season of 1990 or 1991, one of my favorite shows was "The Prince of Belair" with Will Smith. "Roseanne" and "Full House" were also very popular shows.

It was a frigid winter. My girls and I lived on Aqueduct Avenue. Our apartment was on the 1st floor, and we did not have a Christmas tree. Angela and Genevieve wanted a real tree. I had, to my name, twenty dollars. My hope was to buy a little tree for five dollars. My neighbors Ann and Teresa (Ann's daughter) laughed their heads off. They said, "Are you kidding me? You expect to buy a real Christmas tree for five dollars? It won't happen, okay?" I asked Ann if she would send her 15-year-old daughter to help me. "I'm going to need some help," I said. She sent Teresa with me, even though she didn't think I needed help. I anxiously left the building and practically ran to Kingsbridge Road. I thought I would get there before Christmas trees started to run out because it was almost Christmas Eve.

When we got to Kingsbridge Road, some men were selling trees right in front of some stores or in front of the Kingsbridge Armory. Prices ranged from $50.00, $25.00, $20.00 ... I spoke to one of the men about the hopes of finding a tree for $5.00. He must have thought I was out of my mind. I said, "You know I only have $5.00 to spend on a tree. Even though I have $20.00, every dollar is accounted for."

He just looked at me in amazement but did not say a word. "Oh, there's one," I said. I pointed to a tree no more than 4 feet tall. It is perfect! I reiterated, "I only have $5.00." I really don't know what happened, but the vendor said, "If I can't find enough bills for change, you can have the tree for $5.00." Guess what? I paid $5.00 for the tree. I thought Teresa's jaw would have to be picked up from the ground. We left and walked quickly with the tree down the street, and I was praising God. I said, "You, see? Jesus knows how much I can pay. I told you!"

As we walked down the block, carrying the Christmas tree, I thought in my heart, *oh, Lord, how I wish I could have one of those Christmas wreaths they are selling to hang on my door.* No sooner had I thought about it, the same man who sold me the tree for $5.00 yelled down the street to me, saying, "Merry Christmas!" He had not one but two Christmas wreaths in his hand for me, and you know what? They were for free! When I got home with Teresa, I gave her one of the Christmas wreaths to hang on her door.

You see, even the little things you hope for are important to God because they mean something to you. All you must do is believe.

Hebrews 11:1, *"Now faith is confidence in what we hope for and assurance about what we do not see."*

5. You Are Never Left Alone

In the early 1990s, the base age for retirement was 65, and the divorce rate tripled among married couples. It seemed to me that my parents would divorce if something was not done.

Papi left for Cartagena, Colombia, now that he had retired. Mami did not want to leave right away because she wanted to work another year or so.

Papi had a bank account that was falling sideways. There were thousands of dollars he had saved during many years of marriage. Let's say that it was a joint effort. He also had a knack for stocks. I was a little concerned because he and Mami had a joint account. She had equal access to it and knew his intentions of emptying their account and leaving her penniless. However, I did not believe he would do this.

Knowing how much money meant to Papi, I tried to convince Mami to withdraw half of the money and leave him with the other half. After all, he would not have been able to invest and do well without her help. Mami refused, and I was highly upset but did not want any confrontation with Mami or Papi. I guess I was a rebel at home because I could not stand by and watch injustice. Well, guess what he did? He left Mami with one month's rent, and that was all. Mami was devastated! I did not want to say, "I told you so," and so I did not.

A few months passed, and Mami got wind that Papi was dating a younger model, if you know what I mean. Allegedly, he was depressed, and this young lady, according to reliable sources, was consoling him. Relatives knew this woman's reputation as a gold digger! Papi purchased two homes.

Meanwhile, at home, Mami was suffering. We both still lived in the same building on Aqueduct Avenue in the Bronx, on Kingsbridge Road. I lived on the ground floor, and she lived on the fifth floor.

One afternoon, I entered Mami's apartment to see how she was doing, and I found her on the toilet bowl with diarrhea, crying. She could not believe that a man she'd been married to for so many years would be living it up on both of their hard-earned money. My three siblings and I were adults already and were on our own, even though my youngest brother lived with Mami.

The fact of the matter was that Mami should have been enjoying her life with the man she had given her entire youth to. I, for one, was very furious! I wanted nothing to do with Papi.

By the end of the year, I don't know what Papi told Mami, but she was going to retire. I was happy for her. I needed to earn my master's degree before she left. Mami really stepped up to the plate for me, babysitting three nights a week. All I had to do was to leave Angela and Genevieve's dinner ready to heat and serve. Angela was in first grade, and Genevieve was in kindergarten. Mami made sure that they completed their homework and bathed them. Mami told me that I needed to finish my Teacher's Master's Degree in eighteen months, and so I did.

I remember writing my thesis and having to go to the library. One time, Angela and Genevieve got into a cat-and-dog fight in the middle of my research at Herbert H. Lehman College in the Bronx. They had never behaved in that way in public. I had to leave. What an embarrassment!

When Mami could not babysit, I would take them to school with me, and they would sit nicely in class. This class was usually on Wednesdays because their piano lessons were at 7:00 p.m. This meant we had Chinese food on this day, and they would do anything to eat out. Sometimes, it was pizza.

Mami was the only person, except for my mother-in-law, who wanted to make sure my refrigerator had food. Mami worked in the school lunchroom. Sometimes, there were leftover Italian stuffed shells with mozzarella cheese and sauce and leftover milk. This was our dinner.
It was so difficult to go out for anything when winters were very frigid, and it seemed darker at night around 10:00 p.m. on Fridays.

Fast forward, Mami's deadline to finish my master's degree program was a catalyst that compelled me to finish my studies in eighteen months. It really paid off.

I did not want to go to my graduation, but my neighbors and a colleague from my master's program insisted that I attend. They emphasized the fact that Angela and Genevieve needed to see the graduation to show an accomplishment. After all, they attended school with me at times, saw me study, and witnessed the entire process of my research thesis as part of my final assignment.

I realized that this graduation would inspire my girls to do better in life. The graduate procession at City College was very exciting for my girls, Mami, and friends. My mom was the one who helped me become a success. Without her help, I would not have been able to complete my master's degree. She gave me a deadline, and I made it! I was a size two after this ordeal, and my shoulders looked like soap dishes.

What was amazing was that by the grace of God, I was able to cook, bake, sew dresses for my girls, sing in the church choir and still give my girls quality time when I did not have to attend evening classes.

Mami moved to Cartagena, Colombia, to be with Papi for a while. Mom did not leave me alone.

John 14:18, *"I will not leave you as orphans; I will come to you."*
Hebrews 11:1, *"Now faith is confidence in what we hope for and assurance about what we do not see."*

6. Co-op Miracle

During H.W. Bush's presidency, the average price for a brand-new car was about $15,000. Some popular family programs were "Growing Pains," "A Different World," and "Full House."

Around 1987, I was still living at 2609 Aqueduct Avenue but wanted to move out. Members of my family had applied for an apartment at the Amalgamated Co-op. My aunt already was a tenant with a beautiful apartment. My sister and two of my aunt's children had also applied. It was difficult to get in because many people wanted to move here. It is a wonderful place to live.

Many people told me that it could take a couple of years before your application is processed due to the high demand in such a lovely neighborhood.

I told my aunt that even though I was the last one to apply, I will get in before anyone else. My aunt said, "I don't doubt it."

It was too bad that I did not feel safe on Aqueduct Avenue anymore. My job was three blocks down from my apartment. I used to go home for lunch and was able to put up the laundry or the dryer. Apparently, this created a pattern, and a man who was not an angel on my block, made it his business to be across the street from my apartment when I went home for lunch. I thought nothing about it until it became a daily habit. I did not feel safe. I spoke to a close neighbor of mine to tell her husband to speak to the guy because they were acquaintances. Her husband told the male suspect to leave me alone. I was also advised not to go home for lunch anymore.

I needed to get out of this situation. Being alone with two small girls made me very vulnerable.

Prayer was constant. Then suddenly, I thought about going to the co-op to see if they would consider my application since I was so desperate. They stated that there was a waiting list. This is normal, and they were just following the rules.

During my girls' piano lessons, I spoke to Ms. Mabel Gerber, the piano teacher, about my situation and how I was concerned about the safety of my family. She came up with a solution.

She said, "Write a letter to the Amalgamated Co-op and inform them about how you have a vested interest in the community because you teach in the district and that you attended high school and college in the same district."

I made a trip to the co-op office and left the letter. Ms. Gerber told me to make sure that I gave the letter to the right person.

I prayed over this. Not too long after, I received a phone call to see a two-bedroom apartment. Boy, was I over the moon! I was called before my sister, but then, she was called. There was a school up the block for the girls if I wanted them to attend.

In short, we moved in, and it was great! What a blessing. Sometimes, you need more than prayers. You need work too. Faith and work go together.

James 2:14, *"What good is it, my brothers and sisters, if someone claims to have faith but has no deeds?"*

7. The Stoop

In the 1990s, NYC had the largest population of students attending public school in the nation. Per-student spending was on the rise.

The N.Y.C. theater had a great opportunity to rise from its beautiful ashes because its environment improved from X-rated movies, pimps, and bro-ken-down movie houses to magnificent places for elegant shows. Just to mention a few, there were: "Sunset Boulevard," "Miss Saigon," "The Phan-tom of the Opera," and more.

The United States was blessed with very talented female artists from dif-ferent genres who stood out amongst other artists. Shania Twain, Gloria Estephan, Celine Dion, Mariah Carey, and too many to name. Let's just say there was a myriad of talent.

Nothing is more beautiful than a blue sky with the sun beaming down on you, and fresh air hitting your face. It is rejuvenating and refreshing. The same feeling is evident, whether it is winter, spring, summer, or fall.

During my '30s, I had too much energy and just needed an outlet. Perhaps it was the strong, fresh Puerto Rican style coffee I used to make in the mornings. It sort of stayed in my system the entire day. Running was one way I refreshed myself to relax and zone in on my creator. At least, that is what I used to do early in the morning, afternoon, or evening runs.

One of my favorite runs was on Saturday morning hours. Mami watched my girls while I ran two miles around a reservoir in the Kingsbridge area of the Bronx in New York City.

The sounds of nature I considered to be a reward from above, with the trees surrounding the reservoir, birds chirping, and flowers blooming in the spring. I really enjoyed this scenic route of the Kingsbridge area because I passed neighborhood parks and schools like John Peter Tetard, Herbert Lehman College, P.S. 86, and Walton High School. It was like a journey down memory lane because my family moved from Spanish Harlem on East 108 Street in Manhattan to the Kingsbridge area around late 1972 or 1973.

I was in the habit of talking to Jesus about anything that came to my mind. Some were my achievements, but others were a reflection on life and my dreams. My energy levels were high, and this run helped me to calm down in every sense of the word. I needed this run to help me relax, wind down, and prepare mentally for the rest of the week as a single parent.

One summer, I purchased bicycles for my girls so that they could ride them around the reservoir. I wanted one for myself but could not afford it. However, I saw it as an opportunity to bond with Angela and Genevieve and to build stamina. After all, while the girls rode on their bikes, I had to keep up.

Aah … then, when we arrived home, the girls had breakfast; I would make myself a cup of coffee and go to the front of my apartment building in the Amalgamated Co-op housing and pretend I was sitting on a stoop in front of my own house. This stoop was on 80 Van Cortlandt Park South, in the Bronx. It was easy for me to envision this dream in such a beautiful courtyard full of different types of flowering trees and beautiful bushes. I viewed this courtyard as a field of dreams.

This routine went on for seven years and after I married for a second time. My dreams of drinking a cup of coffee on the front steps of my own home did not stop.

The stoop was a place where I dreamed and never gave it another thought. I believed it would happen but did not know or think about how it would happen. I just dared to believe that if I had just a little faith, this dream would also come true! Little did I know this dream was around the corner.

Matthew 17:20, *"He replied, 'Because you have so little faith. Truly I tell you, if you have faith as small as a mustard seed, you can say to this mountain, "Move from here to there," and it will move. Nothing will be impossible for you.'"*

8. Communion Dress

In 1990, some of my favorite movies were "Edward Scissorhands" and "Ghost." In dramas, the "Godfather III" and "Rocky V" were very popular. These movies are still watched today, like the "Godfather Trilogy." I remember these movies being very popular with my friends and family.

The snow had melted, and the buds on the trees started to show signs of life. The morning air, along with the bright sunlight, reminded me that Genevieve needed a kindergarten graduation dress. Being a single mother of two at the time made it difficult to make ends meet since my girls attended a Christian Academy. Thank God that some anonymous members of our local church decided to sponsor them for half the tuition just as long as they kept their grades up.

Their father had disappeared out of thin air. His family and I feared the worst. Did he die on the streets of New York City? There was no word on him. Genevieve's graduation was around the corner, and I couldn't afford a dress.

Every day, the girls asked for their father. Church members and I prayed for a miracle. We wanted him at Genevieve's graduation. I happened to tell a friend of mine, Sandy, about needing a dress for my daughter's graduation. She invited me and my girls to her house in Long Island. Time was running out, and so I wanted Genevieve to be able to wear the most beautiful dress. There was one thing I did not want—my Genevieve to feel that she was different from other students who had both parents living at home.

During our visit to Sandy's house, she gave us a tour. We discussed Genevieve's graduation dress, and she thought about her daughter's communion dress. It was found in some drawer, and she gave it to me. She said, "You know how to sew. Transform the dress." Immediately, I let my imagination run with ideas. I thought Genevieve, as young as she was, would have a stroke. She said, "Mom, a communion dress for my kindergarten graduation? Are you serious?" I promised I would transform the dress. "It will be the best dress ever. No one will know." I looked at the dress and envisioned what I would do to make it look magnificent! The dress had flowers on the breast; it was snuggled tightly around the waist, bell-shaped below the waist had short sleeves and a ruffled back below the waistline.

When I arrived late that Saturday evening, I put the girls to bed and started to envision the transformation of the dress. I grabbed some paper and planned the changes. The flowers needed to be removed, but I thought I could use them on Genevieve's hair. A French Braid in the middle of her long chestnut brown hair would be perfect, with those artificial flowers adorning both sides of her braid. For the waistline, I sketched on a thick and wide lavender ribbon that would be sewn in as part of the dress, tied to the back. However, I needed to accentuate the ruffles, so I took the same lavender material to create a Spanish look on the back of the dress just like the ones the Spaniards use for Flamenco dances.

I thought of a special material store on Fordham Road in the Bronx to purchase what I needed and went to work that evening on the dress. Genevieve's graduation was less than a week away, and I needed my little girl to feel extra special.

Talking about burning the candle on both ends of a stick, I worked during the day as an elementary teacher and took care of my girls until 8:00 p.m., and then went to work on that dress. Three nights gave me the results I wanted from the sketch. Genevieve was so happy!

On graduation day, I had my neighbor, Eva, braid her hair. I could braid hair, but Eva was an expert. She added the flowers from the communion dress on both sides of my little girl's French Braid just as I had envisioned it.

When we arrived at Genevieve's graduation, there was still no sign of her father Ray. It was as if the earth had swallowed him up. My in-laws arrived and sat at the table with me, Eva, and her girls.

Genevieve's dress was the talk. It was amazing, and she looked amazing. Angela, my eldest daughter, called her The Southern Bell. Even though one mother was a seamstress and had made her daughter's dress, she wanted Genevieve's dress. As a matter of fact, all the girls in Genevieve's class wanted her dress. There was so much excitement about the dress that it did not matter that Ray had not shown up. Genevieve felt loved and special that day.

Over the years, I found the communion dress and decided to give it away for another little girl to wear. After all, Genevieve was now a grown woman who still remembers that dress and still complains about me giving it away. "Why did you give it away, Mom? When I have a little girl, I want her to wear it." I did not know how a hand-me-down could be so meaningful. It was the love I put into the dress. This is what Genevieve remembers and how special she felt.

Do Not Worry- Matthew 6:25, *"Therefore, I tell you, do not worry about your life, what you will eat or drink; or about your body, what you will wear. Isn't life more than food, and the body more than clothes?"*

9. Embrace Changes

David Dinkins was the mayor of New York City, and George H.W. Bush was president of the United States. Some of the best female and male artists were Janet Jackson, Mariah Carey, Mickael Jackson, Eminem, Bob Dylan, Celine Dion, and Beyonce.

One late afternoon, I bumped into one of my colleagues from P.S. 86 at a Kingsbridge bus stop in front of a pizza establishment at the time. I was waiting for the Co-op City bus with my two girls Angela and Genevieve. She said, "Elsie, come back. I am sure that you can get a job."

Eventually, I returned to P.S. 86 to visit with my girls, to say hello to staff members and see what would happen. One of the assistant principals was very welcoming and offered me a position at the school.

This happened so long ago, but I remember teaching first grade and kindergarten. Teacher support at P.S. 86 was phenomenal!

Meanwhile, there were plans for a new building to be constructed in the school backyard. It was like a little red schoolhouse for kindergarten and first grade only. Teachers were chosen by the administration. The school's opening made the news. It was like working in the suburbs. Every class had an adjoining bathroom, a sink, cubbies, and a brand-new piano. It was a teacher's dream!

Everything was great! Teachers in this building had a staff developer at their beck and call for any pedagogical practices and even personal issues. It was like having a personal coach. Teachers met every morning over coffee. Everyone pitched in for the coffee, and Mrs. M. Gelfand, our staff developer, made the coffee. We even had lunch together in a multipurpose room. Professional conversations about curriculum and performances were connected to the curriculum.

Our staff was diverse. The safety agent always made sure I ate. He thought I was too skinny. Jose was his name. What a blessing!

Teachers planned together using themes as a guide and put on shows. There was music, art, and learning centers for all subjects. Colleagues celebrated each other's achievements. When I graduated from my first Master's in Early Childhood, I was asked to stop by the school with my cap and gown so that my colleagues and students would celebrate my achievements. One of my colleagues was so excited that she said, "You did it!"

Up to this point, all was good. One day, I was informed that our principal, Dr. Raymond Osinnoff, was retiring. I knew that the school would not be the same. I will just leave it at that. I knew that it was time to leave.

A former teacher who had left the school offered me a position as a bilingual staff developer in another district, so I took a risk. After all, it was a new adventure. What an adventure this opportunity turned out to be! It was not a nice place to work, I soon learned. You could not even get sick! There was a huge scandal at the school that made the newspapers at the time. There was just too much drama for me. I did not know what this whole scandal was about, and I sure did not want to find out or have anything to do with it. My girls Angela and Genevieve were about 7 and 8 years of age, and the ride to my job was longer; I had to get out. Fortunately, I was able to speak to someone who knew the principal personally and mentioned that I had to leave because of family hardship. This allowed me to seek employment elsewhere without burning bridges.

On my way home one day, the sight of a school caught my attention on the Grand Concourse and Kingsbridge Road. It was P.S. 246, The Poe Cottage School. Every day I passed by this school on the bus, I thought, this *school is just ten minutes away from my co-op apartment in the Amalgamated housing.* I began to claim this school to God as my new place of employment. Every time I passed by on the bus, I envisioned myself bringing in my resume and giving it to someone of authority. Well, one day, it happened. I had the courage to prepare my resume, get off the bus, and cross the street. I made it to the school's entrance and climbed the stairs just in the nick of time. There was a man standing by the entrance in a suit, and he asked me if I needed help. I said, "I am looking for a position as a teacher." He accepted my resume and introduced himself as the assistant principal. He said he would get back to me, and he did. I got a job! This school was amazing too. I spent eleven years at this school until my next assignment.

It is okay to dream, imagine, expect, or believe what you imagine, even though you may not know when or how. Just believe! Claim God's promises, and He will hear you. Don't doubt.

Isaiah 41:13, *"For I am the LORD your God who takes hold of your right hand and says to you, Do not fear; I will help you."*

Jeremiah 29:11, *"'For I know the plans I have for you,' declares the LORD, 'plans to prosper you and not to harm you, plans to give you hope and a future.'"*

10. School Crossing

By 1992, The Mall of America opened its doors to the public in Minnesota. Timberlands, scrunchies, Bomber jackets, and chain wallets were part of the fashion statements. Some of the most popular dances were the Macarena, the Electric Slide, and Hip Hop.

No one ever knows why people cross their path in life. Life has many turns and surprises.

I spent at least eleven years at P.S. 246 in the Bronx on the Grand Concourse. It was a wonderful place to work. Teachers and administrators were very collaborative.

Every member of our school was valued. The lunchroom staff and the paraprofessionals were helpful, resourceful, and knowledgeable.

The kitchen staff used to place my pies prepared in class with my students in their ovens during the fall season. We made apple pies, cranberry sauce, apple sauce, and popcorn.

On cold days during the fall, I remember crossing the street with my first-grade class to buy apples and who-knows-what-else at the farmer's market. Students were able to see and purchase some of the harvest products we sang and read about at school. I wanted school to be hands-on and fun. This meant the class and I baked apple pies, fried pumpkin seeds, made applesauce and cranberry sauce after these purchases.

Our school crossing guard made sure that all students were safe, especially crossing over to the farmer's market across the street from the school. On very cold days, I would tell her, "It is too cold out here. Perhaps you should go to school and become a teacher." I spoke to her several times about this, even when she was in the school building.

Fast forward about twelve years or so, I was now working in a middle school in sixth grade. During our school orientation and professional development, the staff was introduced to new teachers on board. I met a teacher I took a liking to. She had a lot of passion and was eager to teach to make a difference. The administration made us a team in an English as a New Language educational program for new students who were at a primary level. I was blessed with working with her. She kept telling me that she knew me from somewhere but could not figure it out. I did not remember her either.

Ms. Colon was a blessing in our class. She was a specialist, and I was the co-general education teacher. Our class was the Tower of Babel, so to speak. We learned from each other. It was a metamorphosis! Ms. Colon brought fresh ideas and innovation, and I shared every practice I had learned throughout the years.

In one of our conversations, she remembered me. She said, "You are the teacher at P.S. 246 who used to tell me to become a teacher. I am the school crossing guard." Then I remembered. So many years had passed, and I had worked in other schools as a coach, assistant principal, and an inclusion class teacher in a middle school/high school setting. Those experiences were a blessing in pedagogical practices.

Ms. Colon is currently an English as a New Language coordinator at Junior High School Herman Ridder 98 in the Bronx.

Isn't it amazing how our Lord works? The very person I recommended to teaching would be a blessing not only to students but to me as well. No one ever knows why people may cross their path. I was fortunate to know why. Life has many turns and surprises.

Hebrews 13:16, *And do not forget to do good and to share with others, for with such sacrifices God is pleased."*

Chapter Eight

1. A Heart Was Touched

In 1989, I did not feel safe in New York City.

Around 1989, when I was approximately 32 years old, I needed a car. By now, both of my girls were attending a Christian Academy in Manhattan.

My children were safe, happy, and were learning a lot. It was my local congregation who provided my girls with a scholarship as long as they kept up their grades. An anonymous church member was paying for most of the tuition.

Since I had an old car, I ran it to the ground because I used it for everything. I used it for shopping, trips to the parks in the suburbs, rides to church for some of the parishioners who attended my congregation, and piano lessons for my girls.

When my car died the first time, one of my neighbors fixed it for me, and then it lasted a while. He and his wife attended the same church. They were very generous and kind. Most of the time, I did not have to shop for new clothes because they gave me hand-me-downs in mint condition for my girls.

I was able to ride the car for a while. However, one day, on a visit to Long Island, the car had about enough. It died in the middle of the highway. My neighbor and our four girls were in the car, and I did not know what to do. A man on the highway stopped and made a call from a cell phone. Now, this cell phone was one of the first cell phones one could have installed in a car. Let me put it this way: if you had a cell phone in your car, you had some money. My car was totaled. What now?

Since it was still summer, my mother, neighbors, and I walked from 2609 Aqueduct Avenue on Kingsbridge Road in the Bronx to our church on 205 Street in Manhattan. It was a great exercise, and we did this every Sunday and, sometimes, for Wednesday night prayer meetings. Sometimes, members from our church gave us a ride.

One day, I began to feel pain while walking. My toes hurt! I couldn't understand why. I was not aware at the time, but I had hammertoes. I ignored the pain and purchased other shoes as a remedy for this situation. I was in the habit of buying the best shoes because I worked on my feet, but this was not working. This discomfort went on for months. Finally, one day, I decided to do something about this unbearable situation.

One day, I overheard one of my colleagues at work talk about a foot doctor who fixed her toes. As a matter of fact, she showed some members of our staff the work of art. It seemed as if this doctor had a great reputation. I inquired about it and didn't care if I had to pay for most of the expenses because this was a private practice, and my insurance would not absorb all the costs. How would I get to this doctor in Pomona, New York? My feet meant a lot! It affected my job and daily activities. Forget about running; it wasn't happening. I had a huge problem—I didn't have a car.

One member of the church got wind of my situation and decided to drive me and did not want me to pay her a dime, not even for gas. I made an appointment with Dr. Barry Schoenberg, the doctor I had heard so much about at work.

All I can say is that this doctor was so attentive to my needs and informed me that my hammertoes could be hereditary. I told him that no matter what shoes I bought, I was in pain. He did his examination and set a date for one of my feet to be operated on. In the meantime, he got to know me, and I shared how one of the local members of the church gave me a ride because I no longer owned a car because I was a single mother of two girls.

Doctor Barry Schoenberg is compassionate and caring. He operated on one of my feet and gave me specific instructions. I was to keep my foot up, take medication, and return for a follow-up. It was a long process because I had to wear a special shoe when I was ready to return to work.

My kindergarten students were wonderful because the paraprofessional had informed them about my operation, and they were careful not to step on me.

After some time, I had to return to get my other foot done. My ride could not make it because she had other matters to attend to. She was great!

I approached another member of the church, and she accepted. She did not want to accept any money or favors for her service either. Again, I went to the office to get my second operation. I was so relaxed that while I looked at magazines and talked about my life basically, Dr. Schoenberg worked on my toes. It was a great distraction for me because I was relaxed. I went through the same process until my last visit.

The last visit would be a final examination and the cost of the services. I had been leaving minimum payments. Dr. Schoenberg excused himself and said he would be right back with my file to let me know the balance. When he left the examining room, he did not return for a brief period. I started to pray for some miracle that the cost would not be too much for me. I would absolutely keep paying until done. I was just too embarrassed to admit this to the doctor.

When Dr. Schoenberg entered the room with my folder, I said to myself, Oh, *oh. I hope it's not too much.* He looked at me and said something like this, "I was looking at your folder, and I saw that you no longer have a balance." I said, "What?" Tears came to my eyes because I believed that Dr. Schoenberg had been touched by God. I remembered a verse, **1 Peter 5:7**, *"Cast all your anxiety on him because he cares for you."*

2. Dad Returns

In the 1990s, the U.S. Census Bureau concluded that 43% of both men and women divorced between the ages of 55–64. It seems as if long-term marriages are breaking up when couples become empty nesters. Mom and Dad were living separate lives.

Dad retired and went to live permanently in Colombia and was there for a while. Mami was a faithful wife who did not lose hope for his return.

After about three years, Dad returned to New York City on vacation. He returned home to Mami, but she was in the hospital.

Mami continued working, even though she had trouble walking and was constantly falling at work. She had terrible arthritis. What was worse was that she had a history with one of her legs. Many years prior, she broke her leg when she walked into a snow-covered hole on a New York City Street after a hard day's work at a factory in Queens. Mami had to wear a cast for weeks before returning to work and daily activities, and she never recovered. Mami used to tell me that she used to lose her balance and had to be very careful.

At the time, she was working in a school cafeteria and told me she was losing strength on both legs and hands. Her arthritis began to sound degenerative, but she insisted on working. She loved her independence.

One day, at work, Mami tripped right over her feet and had to be rushed to Bronx Lebanon Hospital. From what I recall, she had a very serious operation. My youngest brother, Ernie, never separated from Mami; they lived together. They had a special bond. Let me put it this way: when Mami was sick with a fever for days, Ernie did not leave her side. He was only 9 years old.

When Ernie and I went to the hospital, Mami was all alone. Dad had stopped by to see her but left. Mami was a strong woman, but now, she looked fragile and helpless. My brother and I stayed only for a while because I had left Angela and Genevieve with a neighbor. It was late, and I was concerned someone would break into my car because I left two boxes full of expensive clothes that I was going to drop off at my in-laws' for my husband whom I had kicked out because of drugs.

Ernie and I left about an hour or two later and found that my car had been ransacked.

The following day, I spoke to Dad about taking Mami with him. He said he would think about it. Dad stayed with Mami until she was discharged. He returned to Colombia, and Mami did not see him again until she joined him in Colombia.

My brother and I felt terrible. How can Dad expect Mami to continue working? He still was not sending Mami any financial support. My brother helped to pay rent and made himself available to always help Mami with the groceries or anything else. Mami recuperated and returned to work for a while. Dad would visit several times in a span of about 10 or more years from my point of view.

Proverbs 5:18, *"May your fountain be blessed, and may you rejoice in the wife of your youth."*

3. Mami Returns

In 1994, the "Forest Gump" movie, starring Tom Hanks, cashed in $330 million. The gallon of milk was approximately $1.12. Mary Jane shoes and baggy jeans were part of the fashion favorites.

Around 1994, Mami returned to the United States from Colombia and went to live with my sister. My sister was married with four children in a three-bedroom apartment. It was a very trying time for her. My sister did not believe in making her children responsible for washing dishes or cleaning the house. In other words, it was not mandatory. She believed that we did too many adult chores as children and had other responsibilities that should be for parents and not your kids. Since Mami was set in her traditional ways for raising children, it created tension in my sister's household. Mami would wash the dishes and place a sign over the sink, "Wash if you dirty dishes." Mami even shared this with me and showed me the sign when I was at my sister's house. She said, "Cecilia's kids don't have any responsibilities. She does everything for them." Unfortunately, I had to talk to Mami and say, "Mami, this is her family, and she has her own way of raising her children, and we should not get involved."

I don't remember how it happened, but my sister could not take it anymore because Mami was at odds with my niece and nephews. She asked if I would take Mami in, and I did. Cecilia felt so bad, but she did not like the conflicts between Mami and her kids.

Mami was Mami and only cared about all her kids. However, we were now adults, and she still saw us as her kids. In other words, we didn't grow up. Mami moved in with me and my daughters and had the same conflicts with my girls, but I asked my girls not to argue with Grandma and that I would speak to her about whatever situation that needed to be solved.

One summer, when I was on vacation from work, I was out until 10:00 p.m. with my girls from outside activities. Mami did not want me outside with them late, and I was at least 37 years old. Sometimes parents do not realize you've grown. I was already divorced and alone for almost five years. I did leave my mother with my girls to babysit. She watched them when I went food shopping for about two hours. She was a great help. I didn't take advantage of her because she was *Abuela*—Grandma. I wanted her to go and come as she pleased. She loved to go to the park and sit with friends or do her crossword puzzles. Mami was also able to visit her sister because she lived in the same co-op. Sometimes she visited my father's cousin in Manhattan. This made her happy.

One of the things Mami and I had in common was the **Novelas,** Soap Operas in Spanish. We really enjoyed this. I loved speaking in Spanish with Mami. The Spanish language is rich in idiomatic expressions, and it's just powerful. We also spoke a lot about Papi and what happened in Colombia. She was very sad, and I really understood her feelings because Papi had the best years of her life, and now she was penniless while he enjoyed their finances with a younger model. One can only imagine the hurt and abandonment she felt. Mami was the kindest person you could meet, hardworking, totally harmless, and loyal.

Mami became very difficult to live with and did not want to obligate my father to send her money or report him for spouse support. I was financially strapped and asked my siblings to chip in $20.00 a week to help Mami with her expenses. I told Mami that since she did not want to make Papi responsible for taking care of her financially, she should apply for Medicare and food stamps because I could not afford her health care. I tried to use my medical coverage and found it was financially impossible to pay. Reluctantly, she applied.

About a year or so later, Mami moved in with my aunt, and there were conflicts there too. What now? My sister and I talked about buying Mami a Co-op apartment because this apartment was subsidized by the government. We each gave a fair share and took turns making Mami dinner. She was very happy with her ground-floor studio apartment. There was independence, and now the children had a better relationship with Mami. Unfortunately, after a year, I began to understand Mami's obstinate behavior.

Leviticus 19:32, *"Stand up in the presence of the aged, show respect for the elderly and revere your God. I am the Lord."*

1Peter 3:8, *"Finally, all of you, be like minded, be sympathetic, love one another, be compassionate and humble."*

4. The Bahamas

By 1995, Bill Clinton was president of the United States. Some popular songs were "Colors of the Wind" by Vanessa Williams, "Fantasy" by Mariah Carey, and "Secret Garden" by Bruce Springsteen. A gallon of gas was about $1.09, and New York City was considering school all year round.

In the summer of 1995, I worked in the summer school program to earn a trip to the Bahamas with my girls.

I spent at least three or even four hours at a travel agency, making sure I had a hotel stay with two meals a day, shows, and tour sites for the entire stay. It was so late that when my girls and I left the travel agency, it was nighttime.

The morning of our departure, there was a change of seats. Apparently, the travel agency made a mistake on the airplane tickets, and we ended up going first-class. Genevieve practically threw up the first hour. My girls felt like two princesses. This is exactly how I wanted them to feel.

When we arrived at the hotel, we toured the hotel area and planned for Hartley's Underwater Sea Walk or something like that. It was a yacht ride to somewhere in the ocean where we had the opportunity to get a mini lecture on how to walk on the ocean's seabed, how to follow the instructor and be safe. After the lecture, I thought, *Did I make the right decision taking this trip to the middle of nowhere in the ocean?* Now, I was scared and started to panic but did not show it. I prayed we would all be safe. I mean, I wanted my little girls to see another world under the water, and we did.

All three of us went together underwater and saw the most beautiful sites. We all wore a huge helmet that has the same effect as a cup upside down in water and does not let the water in. That was the scary part, but all was well. We even took pictures.

Swimming with the dolphins was another trip we took, but my girls swam, and I did not. It cost an arm and a leg, but it was rewarding to see my girls and other children enjoy dolphins.

We also went sightseeing to a place where slaves built a wall called "The Queen's Staircase" in Nassau, Bahamas. It is a magnificent structure! The stairs are steep and considered a landmark. These steps were named after the late Queen Victoria, who reigned in Britain for 64 years.

One of the attractions at the hotel was a dinner and a show where I saw mostly European families with their children. I was excited for my girls. It was the first time we attended a dinner show.

Every day, we saved some of the breakfast and placed it in the refrigerator because paying for three meals would have been more expensive. We had the leftover breakfast on the beach while we watched people ride on jet skis on the surface of the ocean. It was too expensive for us to ride.

On one of our beach days, we met a man named King, who offered jet skis rides. I told him that I would love to ride, but it was too expensive for me and my girls, so we watched.

One evening at the hotel, my girls were hungry for dinner, so we went to the dining room prior to our reservation. People in front of us were turned away because they were scheduled for later. The maître d'hôtel of the restaurant took one look at me, and I said, "We are not scheduled, but my girls are hungry." We were allowed in, and no questions were asked. Angela and Genevieve wanted Pesto, but it was not part of the menu, so they asked the head waiter to ask the chef if he would prepare it for them. Long story short, they went to the kitchen, and the chef made exactly what they wanted, Pesto! A gentleman sitting across our table, on a date, found them so cute he sent two virgin Shirley Temples to our table. He must have been loaded because he had flown his date over for dinner from either New York or another Island.

The Bahamas is a very friendly and family-oriented place for vacation. People at the hotel saw that I was a single parent and really catered to our needs. This was evident during a Bahama Mama dance contest. Angela and Genevieve wanted me to enter the contest to win some Bahama bags and other prizes, so I did. I could not compete with people who were so drunk they made people laugh, plus I felt a little uncomfortable moving my booty all over the place to win a prize.

A young woman and her father won because they were so hilarious. A parade followed, but the men in charge of the contest waited for the parade of people who were at the contest to leave and called me and the girls to get the Bahama bags anyway. They wanted my girls to feel like I won because they knew I entered the contest upon their request.

On our last day in the Bahamas, we sat at the beach as always, watching people ride on the jet skis. This time, however, the man we met previously asked if we wanted a free ride since we were leaving. All three of us got on his jet ski. It was as if the ocean water looked like a floor made of glass and we were walking on it. What fun! It was an amazing ride, and it didn't cost us a dime.

Ecclesiastes 8:15, *"So I commend the enjoyment of life, because there is nothing better for a person under the sun than to eat and drink and be glad. Then joy will accompany them in their toil all the days of the life God has given them under the sun."*

Chapter Nine

1. My Knight and Shining Armor

Dating in the nineties was different. Adults and teens had extensive conversations on the phone. Some people believed that if you spoke for two or more hours, it was probably the beginning of something serious or love.

Beautiful were the songs of the birds and the warm sun on a Saturday afternoon as I carried heavy grocery bags from the supermarket to my co-op apartment in the Bronx.

"These bags are so heavy; God help me. Where is this man I have been praying for? I know that he is close by, BUT WHERE IS HE?" Thank God no one could hear me. The courtyard was in full bloom, and all seemed serene. There wasn't a soul anywhere. Mom was upstairs with Angela and Genevieve, my daughters. I believe it was summer or late spring when I came boldly to the throne of God. Little did I know that the charming prince I was talking about was around the corner. Yes, he was literally around the corner. Auntie's apartment was right across the street from my courtyard. Isn't it ironic that I lived in another neighborhood, and my aunt happened to be across the street like when we lived in the same building on Sedgwick Avenue, and then across the street from each other on Fort Independence?

Anyway, I quickly made it home to Mami because Angela and Genevieve were with her for about two hours, and I did not like to take advantage of my mother. Grandmas are for spoiling their grandchildren and not permanent caretakers. At least, this was my point of view.

Not long after, on a great sunny day, I was filled with excitement about a new day. Summer cleaning was here again, and I needed to go over everything my girls would not use. Every single drawer in their room was checked for size, wear, and tear. All was okay until I hit the bookshelf full of books. I knew my girls had outgrown them and were well over age. I looked at every single baby book, easy books I read to them, songbooks, and more. I thought I would save them just in case I would have another child. Maybe I would have another girl or a boy. Sadness came over me, but I thought about how fortunate I was to have two girls. If God did not send another child, I would trust Him and thank Him for the treasures I already had. Besides, how was I going to have another child without a husband?

I was a single mother now for over 6 years, and my knight in shining armor had not arrived yet. I thought, *If I couldn't have any more children, let me give these books to my sister's youngest son, who is now about two years old. He can use these books.*

My heart still ached to have more children, but I quickly dismissed the idea when I thought about the joy these books would bring my nephew.

Suddenly, it was fall, and I went shopping one evening when I decided I would stop by my Titi's house so she could watch Angela and Genevieve while I shopped. There was an old friend of the family who had known my family for three generations. Her name is Anna, but everyone calls her Coqui—like the coqui, a frog that can be found in Puerto Rico and can only survive in Puerto Rico. Puerto Ricans just happen to give people some unusual names of endearment that make no sense. I knew her, and she knew me. I mean, this lady knew my great grandmother from Puerto Rico, my mom, and her entire family. As a matter of fact, her father and my grandfather were drinking buddies. God only knows that they both just loved women.

Anyway, the man I would fall madly in love with was coming to pick up Coqui, his mother. Papo, her son, always picked her up. What is funny is that in all the years I knew the family, I only knew of his existence and never met him. Going back to the early eighties, he often went to my Titi's house in another apartment she had, and I always missed him by a couple of minutes either to pick up his mother or his grandmother. Fast forward, getting back to what I was saying, he comes to pick up Coqui, and she volunteers him to take me to the supermarket. I did not know what to say. "Oh, it's nothing! Papo doesn't mind," she said.

We get downstairs, and then Coqui asks me to sit in the front seat with Papo. I start to look at him from the corner of my eye and see he is strong, tall, with dark hair and so handsome. As soon as we got to the supermarket, I said goodbye, and again, Coqui volunteered herself and came into the supermarket to help me shop and then said, "Papo won't mind waiting." I just could not believe that this was happening. I said, "You don't have to. I really hate to make him wait," but Papo said, "It's okay; I will wait." We go to the supermarket, and I am running through the aisles as if the fire alarm has gone off, and the entire supermarket had to be evacuated. Coqui looked at me and asked, "Why are you in such a rush?" I said, "I feel so bad he is waiting outside." Coqui then said, "Don't worry; he's got this girlfriend that is milking him for every penny he has." I turned to her and said, "I know that God will answer your prayers, and he will leave her, or she will leave him. It sounds like a bad situation."

When we left the supermarket, they drove me home. I usually dragged 7–10 grocery bags where I could see them until I got to the elevator and got them upstairs. After all, he had waited for me to shop, and I surely did not expect him to help me. To my surprise, he got out of the car and helped me with my groceries all the way up to my door. I was in love.

A couple of days later, Papo spoke to his mom, Coqui, to ask my Titi to get my phone number, of course, with my mother's approval. He called my Titi and asked her if it was okay to call me. She gave him the green light and the blessing. We spoke several times before even dating. You see, Titi was the matriarch of our immediate family. She was also my mentor and assured me that he was a wonderful man.

Titi always told me that she knew him before he was born. "I saw him grow in his mother's belly, and he is a great match!" she said.

One day, my phone rang on an August day, and it was Papo. We spoke extensively for about an hour or so. He asked me on a date, and it was the beginning of a lovely relationship. He did not mind my already made family, and he had background knowledge about my fear of men at the time and how I had been celibate for seven years. Who do you think told him? It was Titi, of course.

Although my mom did not like the idea of me ever remarrying, it was okay. However, in the past, she would tell me how terrible it would be for me to remarry because I would have another name, and any children I would bear would have a different last name. Anyway, how are you going to ever meet anyone if you never go out anywhere? "Where will you meet this young man, you hope to meet?" she would ask. I would simply say, "I will not have to look because the man that God sends me will knock on my door." Sure enough, after a couple of weeks of conversations after that fall day of shopping, one evening, Papo knocked on my door to pick me up on our first date.

My knight in shining armor was a gentleman in every sense of the word, and he did knock on my door. I did not have to look.

Hebrews 11:1, *"Now faith is being sure of what we hope for and certain of what we do not see."*

2. Scandal

In 1995, "The Riverdance," an Irish and music dance show, opened for the first time on February ninth in Dublin, Ireland, with Michael Flatley as the lead dancer. Science made a breakthrough when a blind teenager from Washington received a bionic eye on March 4. Jerry Lewis raised $47,800,000 for his 30th Muscular Dystrophy Telethon on September 4. The cost of living had begun to be expensive for me. The average income was about 36,000.00. The monthly rent was about $550.00, and a U.S. Postage Stamp was 32 cents.

Life was good. The man of my dreams appeared. Papo and I did not follow the proper way of marriage. As a matter of fact, we did everything backward. I remember talking to God in my backyard as I was struggling to carry my groceries. "**Where is this man?**"

We dated several times. Papo was a complete gentleman. My sister would babysit, or sometimes, my mother would babysit. After around three or four dates, my brother-in-law suggested that my daughters should also join us on our dates. I did not want to introduce them yet because it was too early in the relationship. I turned to my mother, and she made the same comment. When Papo asked me on another date, I was a little uncomfortable asking him permission to bring my girls along. He did not mind at all. Papo realized I was getting push-back from my family. It seemed that my sister, in good faith, had a talk with my mother about not babysitting because the girls had to get used to another man in their lives. They had, I believe, good intentions, but it was bad timing.

Papo was so generous and so kind that he welcomed the idea. Little did I know that he had had previous experiences with dates who had children.

So, what I viewed as being pushy was normal for him. Papo began to integrate himself into my family slowly. It began with the movies, followed by driving me to Bainbridge for my girls' piano lessons. The girls also had dance lessons at the Bronx Dance Academy.

We moved in together, which was not right, got pregnant, and then got married. What a scandal! I felt guilty because I knew that God did not approve of this behavior. My mother did not want me to marry anyone else. She said, "You should not marry again. It is awful to give your kids a stepfather and bear children with another name. This is terrible. I only had one man in my life."

Can you imagine what happened when my bump showed up? I was now 39 years old and living in sin! Papo belonged to another denomination and kept traditions of religion different from mine. This caused a lot of friction, which I also felt guilty about.

It was not easy. The girls had to adjust to a new male figure in their lives, and many family members had a lot to say. It was either for or against. I had been a single parent for 7 years and did not date. To me, this was a time to reflect on the past. I did not want to repeat a vicious cycle that countless women face when dating or marrying another man. Many women who decide to fill in a void find themselves in the same situation, and this is what I wanted to avoid.

My mother knew about Papo and I living together and about a baby on the way. She kept this secret from the rest of the family, except for Titi, my aunt, who knew. You see, Titi knew about Papo from the time his mother announced her pregnancy. As a matter of fact, Papo walked on water, and she loved him so much!

Meanwhile, at my sister's workplace, there was a meltdown. I was told by Papo's aunt, who worked at the same school and was a very close friend of the family. Apparently, she was in the staff lounge of the school when my sister started bawling. After all, the family went back three generations from Puerto Rico and then became close friends in New York City. I guess one family followed another to America for a better life.

As I mentioned previously, this is how the Puerto Ricans immigrated to New York—one relative found a place, and then family and friends followed, pursuing the American dream.

Anyway, Titi Lucy thought my sister had lost a member of the family because everyone in the staff lounge witnessed this scene. When Titi Lucy asked what was wrong, my sister said that I was living in sin with Papo. Yes, she was right, but did she have to publicize it in this way? After all, this was a public place of employment.

Titi Lucy said, "Wait a minute. This is my nephew you are talking about, and what do you mean he is living with your sister?" She had no idea that Papo and I had hooked up. Oh, my goodness, what a **bochinche**, gossip, and a disgrace, even though it was well-intended. Yes, I was not living right, but an entire school building, where I once had progressed as a school aide, assistant teacher, and then became a teacher, did not need to know something so intimate.

My aunt was furious! She said, "Why didn't your sister speak to you? She should have shielded you with her skirt!" As a Christian, you are supposed to confront whoever offends you or sins against you, and if they do not listen, you get a witness, and then, if they still don't listen, the church talks to them to try to bring them back to the fold or expel them.

Matters got worse when my sister found out I was with a child. As she left our mother's house, and I stopped by, she demanded to know when I was going to tell her about my pregnancy. I thought to myself, *I am 39 years old, and no one ever came to my house, except for Mami, to see if my girls needed milk, groceries, or even a baby-sister for an emergency. Where were they?*

God is merciful and patient. He forgives us even when we mess up. Yes, there are consequences, but He is so good that He does not give us what we do deserve.

1 Peter 4:8, *"Above all, love each other deeply, because love covers over a multitude of sins."*

3. The Man in a Suit

In 1996, there was a severe blizzard, and schools were closed in New York City. The storm paralyzed the city. The gusts of wind were powerful, and people were stranded. Some people took out their sleds and even their skis.

When we are young, events may happen in our lives that hold no significance. We talk about them and ask ourselves questions. However, sometimes, they mean something, and in your innocence, you ignore them. After all, what would a ten-year-old think and dream about? They dream about conversations, television shows that they watch, or even re-live a situation they had during the day—and dream about it at night. This is quite normal for anyone.

One night, as I slept, I dreamed about a huge party but did not know where I was or who was there. I did know there were a lot of people invited. It seemed like I was in a living room full of people. The colors were a combination of beiges and light browns. The time of day felt like an evening of family and friends at a party. I found myself dancing with someone much taller than me. It could have been anybody! I was not a little child but a grown woman. I thought nothing about it. I remember seeing the profile of a man but could not distinguish who he was. I did know that he was tall, fair, had black hair, and wore a black suit. I could really see half his face, but that was all. What could this mean? You know what? I said, "This is just another one of those random dreams one has" and did not give it another thought. Nonetheless, the dream was so vivid that I never forgot it.

Fast forward 29 years later, there was a party just how I had described it. It was my first dance with the man of my dreams. I immediately thought of the dream when he held me in his arms. It was the man in the black suit, and I could see half of his face. It was the man I had married.

The bridal party was at my husband's house. It was full of family and close friends in my husband's apartment in Co-op City. The shades were beiges and light browns. Family and friends watched and clapped as we had our first dance as a married couple.

With God, anything is possible. I was not expecting this event but wondered.

Jeremiah 29:11, *"For I know the plans I have for you,' declares the Lord, 'plans to prosper you and not to harm you, plans to give you hope and a future.'"*

Chapter Ten

1. The Boy Without a Voice

The late 1990s was a time when more minorities like me became first-time homeowners. Food prices seemed to be more reasonable. The gasoline price was about $1.23, and the cost of a gallon of milk was about $2.41.

There were wedding bells for me! I was married in June of 1996, and by December, guess what? A baby wanted to jump out of my womb. Unfortunately, my life was all backward. Nonetheless, a child was on the way. During this pregnancy, my students sometimes had celebrations in the classroom, and there were mothers who were professional bakers from the Dominican Republic. They made the most delicious cakes. I ate so many of these cakes that after the baby was born, I could not look at another cake for two years.

Angelo is my firstborn son but was my third child. He had his paternal great-grandmother's eyes, and he also mirrored my eldest daughter in every sense of the word. I told my husband, Papo, to allow me to name him. I thought of the name before he was born and decided to name him after his eldest sister Angela; I named him Angelo De Jesus. This meant that **he was an *Angelo***, an Italian word for Angel, because he belonged to Jesus. His eyes just happened to be hazel green just like his sister's. The only difference was that Angela's were a deeper green, and she had a black birthmark on one of her eyes like my Colombian paternal grandfather.

As Angelo grew, he was very active and did not like to take naps or even sleep at night. When he was about 5 months old, he cooed and always smiled. Angelo was a very happy baby with a wonderful disposition. He was about 6 weeks old when my mom began babysitting. She simply adored Angelo. Since Abuela lived on the ground floor, Angelo said hi to everyone who went by her ground floor apartment window. Since my firstborn Angela and Genevieve were born overseas, Grandma did not get to really enjoy the first few weeks of their births like she did with Angelo.

Meanwhile, my family was growing very uncomfortable in our co-op apartment after two baby showers; we ran out of room. It seemed as if Angelo was a good reason to find more space in a bigger apartment or a house with two teenage girls. One thing I did notice was that Angelo did not try to say mama or papa. Months just zipped away, and all I heard were grunts. It was obvious that Angelo had good receptive language because he pointed to objects or food, and I would name them to see if he would repeat. Nothing!

House hunting was terrible. I made appointments to see different prospects for a house but could not find anything until I met this real estate agent, Pearl. She was very accommodating and very understanding. We moved upstate, and Abuela would come for the week to babysit Angelo and go home on Friday to return on Sunday.

It got to be too much for my mother to care for Angelo at the house. There were stairs with gates, and Angelo would throw pillows down the stairs and then throw himself. Somehow, Abuela was not able to keep up with him. My husband and I decided I would drive Angelo to the Bronx so that Abuela could babysit Angelo in her ground-floor studio apartment and have more control.

Every day, on my way home, I sang to Angelo to keep him happy during an hour's drive. I also wanted to teach him how to talk using songs like "Old MacDonald Had a Farm," "The Wheels on the Bus," and "The Itsy-Bitsy Spider," just to name a few.

Shortly after, my mother was hit by a car and needed almost 24-hour watches, with insurance nurses sent to her house every day. Thank goodness for insurance! Although Mom was recuperating physically, she was deteriorating cognitively. Previously, I noticed Mom had trouble deciding which key to use to open her apartment door and would forget how to place the cast iron grates on the stove, and this troubled me.

Mom loved Angelo so much that we did not know how to tell her she could not babysit. My husband and I decided to look for a nursery upstate close to home to take care of Angelo. I was so concerned about my mother and Angelo, who was now 18 months old and still was not able to communicate effectively with outsiders. Being that I was a teacher, I was worried because I had been a mother two times before, and I knew what children should be able to do at every stage of development.

Fast forward, we found a nursery called Kiddie Connection. I went to an agency in town that informs the community about safety and other matters. They informed me that Kiddie Connection had high reviews.

My daughters and I decided to take Angelo one day to get a feel for it. We toured the place, and Angelo did not want to leave. This was a sign that this was a very inviting place if Angelo wanted to stay.

Angelo started nursery school when he was about two and a half years old. His nursery schoolteachers provided a lot of hands-on interactive activities and noticed that Angelo would not participate. One teacher said, "He understands what we are saying, and we can see in his eyes that he knows what to say but doesn't know how to express what he wants to say. He avoids participation." They stated that he was very guarded in a small group. It was evident to them that he understood all the instructions but avoided any type of communication.

I decided one night that Angelo needed to be evaluated. While giving Angelo a bath, I was in the habit of giving him his vitamin every night like clockwork. However, on this night, I forgot. Angelo was desperately trying to remind me and was getting frustrated and then said, "*vitamina.*" He had resorted to the Spanish word for vitamin. I rarely spoke to him in Spanish, but I knew Abuela spoke to him in both languages. He could not remember the English word, and so he resorted to Spanish. "Oh, my goodness! My son needs a lot of help," I said.

I spoke to my husband about how I wanted Angelo to be tested for speech and language challenges. Coqui, my mother-in-law, who happened to be visiting, said, "When Papo was little, he used to have his own way of communicating, and only I understood him. He used to call his vest, in Spanish, a *cacheton,* which means plump-cheeked, instead of *chaleco.*" Papo chimed in and said, "I think you are exaggerating because you are a teacher. There is nothing wrong with him. I used to go to a speech class when I was in the first grade." Coqui agreed and elaborated on how she was provided with speech services when she was in high school. I immediately jumped on this opportunity and said, "Are you listening to what you are saying? Do you realize that both of you received special education services?"

As a matter of fact, my sister also received services at school, and I complained that I was not getting the same attention she was receiving. "So, there, the entire family is special ed. I am special ed; you are both special ed. I am going to go to Westchester Medical Hospital to have Angelo evaluated. He is smart, and I do not want him to join the countless number of students I have encountered throughout the years who never received these services and were living in a silent world of their own. This means that Angelo would not be successful in reading and writing or in life. I need to rule this out. The longer we wait, the bigger the gap. I do not care if you agree or not. We are not experts, and we need them to decide. I would rather rule this suspicion I have out," I said.

Shortly after, my husband and I went to Angelo's primary physician for his regularly appointed checkup and shared our concerns. One example we shared was how I had to stop everyone at the dinner table from speaking when Angelo was trying to say something; it was like playing Charades. His doctor wrote a request to have Angelo evaluated.

My husband was a little apprehensive about this possible label being placed on his son but agreed because he did not want to hear my mouth if Angelo started school and was singled out as learning disabled.

Westchester Medical Center was phenomenal! They wanted to test Angelo in Spanish first. However, I stressed that Angelo was English dominant but agreed to the testing in Spanish because my mother spoke to him in two languages.

As a result, the bilingual evaluation concluded that Angelo was English dominant and was three and a half years behind in language but was very smart. I immediately said, "I told you something was wrong with my baby." Papo did not dare say a word. The results of Angelo's evaluation began with a meeting with the county to receive speech services.

Speech services, for me, meant learning how to teach in another way. The speech pathologist assigned Angelo homework and taught me how to become an even better teacher because I had to follow up on all the treatments. Angelo was assigned a notebook with an assignment every time she met him. Just to name a few of the assignments, I had to name everything using hands-on visuals for all activities with Angelo. He received services right at the nursery school. Each session was one hour, one on one, and it was intense.

Angelo began exhibiting frustration now that he was almost 4 years old. I had talks with him every day about not putting his hands on anyone, even though he did not. I feared that out of frustration, he would have tantrums, and he did. Whenever the speech pathologist came to the nursery two times a week for an hour, Angelo would miss some fun activities. The teachers would ask each other, "Who is going to tell Angelo that recess is over?" **They called it the wrath of Angelo.** Of course, this statement was not insulting at all because it seemed as if Angelo was calling the shots, having his little tantrums, because he had not developed a bank of words to express his thoughts. That was how he protested. These teachers were so super that they spoke to him and provided other activities to calm him down.

After almost two years of speech, Angelo was 5 years old. He did not have to attend school because he was born in late December and had missed the cut-off date; thank God! I saw this as an opportunity to teach him the basics of reading and writing. My husband and I had to make a big decision. We decided that whoever earned the highest salary would go to work, and the other would stay home. We both cried because I wanted to stay home, and my husband also cried because he was now Mr. Mom. By then, our second son was born, and the cost for nursery care was too much for us. Therefore, I left daily lesson plans for art, math, reading, and writing. Fine motor activities were included because Angelo's writing looked like chicken scratch. It was a very trying time for my husband and me. When I arrived from work, I had to finish the assignments because Angelo fought his father every step of the way. We did not give up! This meant instruction six days a week.

When Angelo went to kindergarten, he was almost six years old. We were very concerned about his social behavior in an academic setting. This was like a test.

During parent-teacher conferences, we met with his teacher. She stated that Angelo was a wonderful boy and a good reader. His teacher said he always had a smile on his face and was very helpful. I said, "Is this my son

Angelo that you are talking about?" I was so happy that tears came to my eyes. I remembered that on one occasion, the speech therapist complained about Angelo's behavior and said he was antsy. All the work we had invested throughout his early life was reaping its benefits.

One turning point in Angelo's educational journey happened in the fourth grade when he came home and had to write an essay. He told his father, "I got this; I can do this alone." We cried at the kitchen table. Angelo felt confident about writing an essay without any support or prompting.

Throughout his early years, Angelo was like the classroom editor, and we still worked with Angelo, even when he attended public school and was placed in an advanced English class. He hated it but then grew to understand our concerns. Angelo used to also participate in community service at a middle school to help boys read, where I was employed as a teacher. They followed his lead and participated in readings. In high school, his counselor said that he had leadership skills in so many words. "Kids follow him."

Angelo found his voice. He was able to express himself not only in writing but also verbally. The silence turned into "Can you please stop talking?" He was able to articulate his thoughts, beliefs, and his personal point of view. He grew to have a heart for students who could not read. We realized this when Angelo came home and was upset and sad over college students in a community college who could not read.

My husband and I helped Angelo in his journey of finding his voice at a very trying time but realized it had many blessings. Angela, our eldest daughter, was so inspired by Angelo's progress that she decided to become a speech pathologist. The funniest thing was, she attended the very medical school in Westchester Medical Center, where Angelo was evaluated, and later, his second sister would attend medical school and become the poster medical student at the medical college.

It is amazing how Angelo, a boy without a voice, could be the very instrument that helped his sisters find their passion in life and equipped me with the tools and strategies necessary to help find the silent voices of all the students in my classroom.

Romans 8:28, *"And we know that in all things God works for the good of those who love him, who[a] have been called according to His purpose."*

2. The Accident

In 1996, the number one song on the billboard was "Macarena." President Bill Clinton was elected for a second term. The standard cost of a television set was about $121.00, and the Nokia Communicator was ahead of its time because people could send emails, browse the web, and more.

By 1996, my third child Angelo was born. My sister suggested that Mami take care of him. She said, "Mami took care of my kids, and now it is your turn." I really thought that was nice because Mami was already taking care of my nephew, Daniel. I believe Daniel, from what I recall, was already attending a nursery school.

Mami was excited because she did not get to babysit my two daughters Angela and Genevieve as newborns because they were born in Germany. She was thrilled that she was going to take care of Angelo. We knew that he would be spoiled rotten. The only condition we set for Mom was that she had to accept payment. My husband and I said, "Just because you are Grandma, it doesn't mean you don't get paid. You must accept the payment. We would have to pay someone else; why not you?" We saw this as an opportunity for Mom to have extra money to buy what she wanted.

As soon as I finished my maternity leave, Mami took care of Angelo when we moved upstate on Columbus Day weekend in 1997. Angelo was about ten months old. Christmas was around the corner, so we decided it was best for Mom to live with us all week and leave with Papo every Saturday on his way to work.

As Angelo grew, he was so active that Mom could not keep up with him. Angelo was fond of flinging pillows over the gate, blocking the stairs. He did it so quickly that Mom would find him down the stairs on the pillows. Angelo knew he would get hurt without the pillows, and this was so obvious. Mom found it difficult to watch him, and we began to suspect something was wrong. Mom did not want to be separated from Angelo; they were a team. They always had a smile on their faces. Mami and Angelo were happy campers.

Since Angelo was a very active toddler, my husband and I decided that we should have Mami take care of Angelo on her ground-floor apartment again. Her apartment faced the front of the building. Angelo said hello to everyone that walked by the window. The window had a window guard and was safe because Mami could play with Angelo, or they watched children's shows like the Teletubbies. Papo sometimes stopped by before me and fell asleep on the sofa. Mom and Angelo would stand in front of him and just laugh at him because his snoring was very loud, and his mouth was wide open. It was as if they were both children enjoying a good laugh.

One day, Angelo wanted orange juice, and Mom decided they would go to a mini market down the block across the street to buy it. I was getting out of my car and saw them crossing the street.
When we got to her front door, I noticed that Mom had trouble deciding what key to use to open her apartment door. I found it kind of strange.
Another time, Mom was washing the stove grates and placed them backward. I told her, and she fixed them. However, she continued to place the grates in the wrong direction whenever she cleaned the stove.

On another occasion, she was cooking chicken thighs, and she called them ticks. She could not remember the word for thighs. It was as if she was lost for words. There was another time when she was watching one of her favorite Spanish talk shows and said that one of the television hosts was talking to her.

I discussed this situation with my husband and took Mom immediately for an evaluation. The doctor informed us that Mom was in the very early stages of Alzheimer's. This was devastating, and I knew that I could not have her take care of Angelo, and that she would need help. When I told my sister, she could not believe it and did not want to accept this terrible news. I understood how she felt, but the doctor was a specialist, and there were no reasons to doubt his prognosis. It was evident to me because of the warning signs. I also shared my observations with my sister. Since my sister was in the same courtyard, she watched over Mom. Her memory was not gone yet, but she became distracted crossing the street one day, and a man put his car in reverse and hit her. Mom tried to tell him to stop, but his music was too loud, and he did not hear her.

She ended up with a cast on her leg and a cast on her arm. A professional nurse came for weeks to clean, cook, and help Mom. By then, I was on summer vacation and came to visit. Mom needed to see Angelo and asked if she could care for him. This was so sad because she couldn't. I told her that Angelo needed to get help in speech therapy and needed to be in nursery school now that he was about three years old.

My sister continued to stop in daily, and eventually, my youngest brother moved in with Mom so that she would not be alone. I continued to visit but was one hour away. No matter how much mom forgot things, she always remembered Angelo, and he always remembered her. They were a team.

Although Mami healed, she was never the same. One weekend, I brought my mother home to see our newborn Marcel. As she walked up the stairs, she and Angelo looked at each other with a smile, a kiss, and a strong hug. She did not forget him or us. My mother-in-law was sitting in the living room, and tears rolled down her cheek at this wonderful sight. Mami spent hours holding Marcel. She loved children; I could not let her miss this occasion. I am so glad we were able to give her happiness while she still remembered.

Mom passed away on August 30, 2004. It was the saddest day for my entire family.

Ecclesiastes 3:1–8,
¹ There is a time for everything, and a season for every activity under the heavens:
² a time to be born and a time to die, a time to plant and a time to uproot,
³ a time to kill and a time to heal, a time to tear down and a time to build,
⁴ a time to weep and a time to laugh, a time to mourn and a time to dance,
⁵ a time to scatter stones and a time to gather them, a time to embrace and a time to refrain from embracing,
⁶ a time to search and a time to give up, a time to keep and a time to throw away,
⁷ a time to tear and a time to mend, a time to be silent and a time to speak,
⁸ a time to love and a time to hate, a time for war and a time for peace.

3. The Miracle No One Expected

Nokia phones were cellular phones in the early 2000s. It was kind of a big cell phone. The average gallon of milk was about $ 2.78, and the average salary was about $30,800.

One never knows how many children God will send. You can only hope that when you believe your time of childbearing years ends, you may find grace again.

Many seasons have passed since my first pregnancy. Eleven years passed before my 3rd child Angelo. Angela and Genevieve had each other because they were about 17 months apart. When Angelo was born, Genevieve was 11, and Angela was 12, and I was 39 years old. I didn't want him to grow up without a sibling close to his age. Angelo was a blessing to the entire family. After all, Papo, his dad, was an only child.

My 40th birthday was approaching, and I didn't want to wait. My husband and I were able to conceive. We were elated! Eight weeks later, we lost the baby. I took a few days off from work to grieve but trusted my Jesus with all my heart. I thought that the loss was meant to be. God never makes mistakes. Perhaps my baby was sick, and God took him home. Who was I to question God? He had already blessed me three times. My doctor said that we could try again.

The next time would be about a year later. My husband and I were over the moon. At the end of the 4th month or so, my family attended our daughters' piano recitals. I will never forget this day because it was June 7, our wedding anniversary. When we left the recital, I was not feeling well and was rushed to the hospital. A technician took a sonogram to see how the baby was doing. I noticed that the screen had no signs of life. I told the nurse; she turned the screen and went to get my doctor. She had no idea I could read the screen. I could see that the baby had not developed. Papo was so supportive. I had to take some days off from work to recuperate mentally and physically. The worst thing was having to explain what happened repeatedly at the job about the loss. It was only normal. People mean well but may not realize that asking the same questions is like opening a wound all over again.

One sunny summer afternoon, when I had dismissed my first-grade class, a parent, whose daughter was in my class, asked about my youngest child, Angelo. She was a kind parent whose daughter was a delight in my class. She said, "You should have another one so Angelo can have a partner." One of my closest colleagues interjected and said, "He may as well be an only child …" I don't remember the rest of the comment. All I know is that it pierced my heart, and I pondered about it. As we carpooled, I did not say a word. I just believed that all things were possible, and I would not give up hope.

Every Sunday, when I went to the Lord's house, I prayed to God for a miracle. My husband, Papo, would look at me; he knew what I was praying for. He never discouraged me.

Fast forward almost two years, I was informed by my gynecologist that I had menopause, and it would be difficult to conceive. However, he ran some tests, and it was confirmed. I was now considered sterile after some hormone tests. I was very pensive. Would you believe that I still did not give up hope?

Meanwhile, I had not been myself. When you work as an early childhood teacher, you can get sick with just about anything in your system. I developed an ear infection, so I had to go to my physician. For some reason, the ear infection was gone, and now my throat was infected. This was kind of strange because I never get sick, and medication always works because I am not resistant to any antibiotics. This only happens when people are constantly taking medication, and this was not my case.

As I waited for my turn to see the doctor, I saw a magazine with a baby on the cover. A little voice in my inner soul said, "Get tested." I thought how ridiculous this thought was. According to the gynecologist and the lab test results, I was sterile, and it was impossible to conceive. When I was called into the doctor's office, I said, "I know this sounds impossible, but my body couldn't fight infection after having taken antibiotics. I don't drink, smoke, or use drugs. I am not resistant to any medication, especially antibiotics. Besides, I went from an ear infection to a throat infection. It is as if something is pulling everything out of me." The doctor listened to me and had me tested. I WAS PREGNANT and had my **menses** for two months in a row! In the Spanish culture, when you are with a child and continue with your menstrual flow, it is called *luna llena*, meaning a full moon. Well, that is what it was, a full moon! Sterile, huh?

We were blessed once again! There were no symptoms but sleepiness and hunger. On one of my regular checkups, my doctor noticed, based on her exam, that I had a lot of amniotic fluid, a little out of the norm. She requested I see specialists at Westchester Medical group for follow-ups. Sure enough, it was as I had been diagnosed. The doctor made a comment about how good my gynecologist was at detecting a lot of amniotic fluid in my uterus.

On one visit, the technician saw a hole in my baby's esophagus. I could see it myself. He immediately called the physician on call to explain. It was not good. My son could be born with problems. It is all a fog right now about what was said. All I remember is that I was afraid.

One afternoon, when Diane, the household service, came and noticed that I was crying, she asked me what was wrong, and I told her. She said, "Do you believe that Jesus can heal?" I said, "Yes, I do." She placed her hand over my belly, and we both prayed that God would heal my son and believed that He did without a doubt.

Two weeks later, I went to my regularly scheduled appointment. When the technician saw the sonogram, the hole in my son's esophagus was closed. He ran out of the office to get the doctor. They invited my husband and me to the geneticist's office for an explanation. I told the doctor, "What are you trying to explain? God has healed my son. There is nothing to say but that God healed my son." She was speechless, and we left. I continued visiting the hospital until June 19, 2000.

It was a beautiful sunny but hot day when I suspected I was in labor. However, when the nurse checked me, she said that I had not dilated enough. When she called my gynecologist, she said, "Do not let Mrs. Martinez leave." She arrived at the hospital, only to realize I had no pain and had to be induced. Had she not kept me in the hospital, I would have died along with my son.

Since I had been in a car accident in my 4th month, I was high-risk. Therefore, I had to have a cleaning service at home and receive physical therapy.

Basically, I could not do anything. This labor lasted at least 11 hours. My doctor had me in every position possible—unimaginable—to get my son out. There were tools that she pulled out that I had never seen. On one occasion, during labor, she asked me to stand on the bed and push down, and my baby would not come out. My son Angelo was born in an hour and a half. My doctor kept saying, "This is not fair."

What was surprising was that on this day and night, no one came to deliver. As a matter of fact, I had my doctor and two or three nurses for myself. They held my hand and rubbed my back. The scary part was when the nurse asked for a proxy. My husband was in the next room with our son Angelo. I started praying, **"Dios mío, yo no me quiero morir. No quiero dejar a cuatro huérfanos."** One of the nurses asked me what I was saying. I said, **"I am asking God to spare my life! I do not want to die and leave four orphans."**

When my husband came into the delivery room, there was blood all over the place, and the nurse was preparing me for a transfusion. My husband yelled from the top of his lungs, "Push him out!" I told my doctor to cut me open. "I don't care if you can't give me anesthesia; just get him out!" I spoke. At this point, pain was the least of my worries.

With that last push, Marcel was born. Would you believe that no one came to deliver until Marcel was born? It was as if God had all His attention on me. Our lives were at risk, and He orchestrated Marcel's safety into this world.

I went home three days after the delivery, and a nurse came to visit me at home to check on us both.

When Marcel came home, he slept all night. I had to wake him up to nurse. He just did not want to be disturbed. Sometimes, I would check to see if he was breathing. It was amazing!

Marcel is a marvelous young man that brought tears of joy from the day he was conceived and came into this world he recognizes as God's creation.

Psalm 138:3, *"In the day when I cried out, you answered me, and made me bold with strength in my soul."*

4. A Rose

Historically, Valentine's Day in America is very important to many couples, whether they are married or just dating. Some surprises could be roses, special chocolates, wining and dining, a romantic weekend, or even a marriage proposal.

February is a holiday many couples make a big fuss about. In some cases, husbands or wives are on their best behavior by doting on their spouse that entire week before the 14th of February. Meanwhile, for the rest of the year, they fight and complain about each other. Most of the time, there is a high expectation of what one may receive from their spouse. Sometimes, their gift is disappointing, and they owe a ton of money.

My husband and I both agreed that on holidays, we would not buy each other any gifts because we could not afford it. The only ones that mattered were the children. This rule applied to birthdays and Christmas.

One Valentine's Day, I arrived home late. As usual, I said hello and went straight to my bedroom. I began to get ready for dinner and put my things away. Dinner was ready because my husband was Mr. Mom, and I, the breadwinner. Dinner was always on time. This was the best we could do for our family.

Later in the evening, the children were already in bed. I went to shower, and when I was ready for bed, I saw this rose on my pillow. I said, "WOW!" I cannot even put into words the feeling of love I felt. It was generous, kind, and romantic. I felt like crying! How could such a small detail really be a big one?

Only true love would see this rose as an enormous gift. You see that the little becomes much when you place them in the Master's Hand?

Psalm 145: *"They speak of the glorious splendor of your majesty- and I will meditate on your wonderful works."*

Chapter Eleven

1. Heritage

In 2004, more women were able to obtain an induced abortion than in the 1970s. Roe versus Wade was in full swing since the 1973 ruling from the Supreme Court. History may have repeated itself in my home if my husband and I would have been judgmental.

One night, Angela and Genevieve came in June to spend time with their brothers who were now four and a half and seven and a half years old. They spent the entire weekend with them in 2004. Genevieve had just ended her first semester at the University of Vermont, and Angela had finished her second year at Vanderbilt University.

The following week, Genevieve came again to visit us. I was in the kitchen when Genevieve told me that she had something to tell me. "Mom, I am about two months pregnant." The baby's father was her high school sweetheart. Whatever the announcement was, Papo, my husband, had a suspicion on the previous visit. He told me that Genevieve's glowing face was of an expectant mother but did not want to share such a thought with me.

Genevieve was 19 years old. This situation gave me a flashback from the past, and I did not want to repeat history. This was an opportunity to give Genevieve all the support I knew I would not receive from my own parents when I found myself in the same situation and got the wrong counsel. Abortion, at that time, was the only counsel I had received from my 35-year-old boyfriend who took advantage of my inexperience, and this includes one of my best friends who did not know any better and gave me the same advice.

Papo and I looked at each other and, in unison, said, "Abortion is not an option." When I and Genevieve had a quiet moment, I said, "Look, we will support you; do not cry. Now, what are you going to do? I am not a babysitter."

Genevieve was under the impression that she and her boyfriend could move into the downstairs apartment and would work in a local restaurant to earn a living. I said, "Absolutely not. You cannot marry just because you are having a baby." At the beginning, she and her boyfriend did not know what to do. Genevieve knew that abortion was not the way to go because of her Christian upbringing, and she did not want this as an option. My husband and I both agreed, "This is a Christian home, and we cannot destroy a human life."

After Genevieve left, we both agreed that marriage was out of the question because they were too young to make a lifelong decision.

Genevieve had all intentions of moving back home. Her aunt agreed. My husband and I, in the meantime, were preparing a room for them, with a brand-new bed for Genevieve. A crib was already in the house because of our two young boys. The room was ready. Somehow, during the months that followed, Genevieve changed her mind and wanted to stay at her aunt Cecilia's house after the baby was born. There was no convincing her. My sister tried to persuade her. She had enough responsibility because her own granddaughter was already under her care. Genevieve's paternal grandmother was very concerned and spoke to me about the current situation. She said, "Elsie, she needs you. You can give her the support she needs." I said that I would continue praying so that Genevieve would return home.

Seven months later, Genevieve gave birth to her son, Jaden. When she laid eyes on her son, she decided to return home as soon as she was discharged from the hospital. My sister packed her bags and her furniture, and my husband went to pick them up.

Genevieve lost her scholarship at the University of Vermont and enrolled at my Alma Mater, Herbert H. Lehman, in the Bronx.

Papo reminded Genevieve during her recuperation period of five months that he would become our grandson's babysitter. She returned to school, and Papo became the sole care provider. Jaden was spoiled rotten. He went everywhere with Grandpa. As he grew, Papo had to chase Jaden out in the fields while our sons played baseball and football. He was a bundle of energy.

In four years, Genevieve graduated from Lehman College and then was trying to find a quick career path so that she could become independent by still working at a local restaurant with our grandchild's father. She thought they could make a living working at a local restaurant business and have her boyfriend move into our house. We were not having it. Genevieve continued seeing her son's father until she met a local resident when waitressing at her place of employment. She dated this young man, who was studying to be a certified accountant. He made a comment to Genevieve about how much doctors made during one of their conversations about careers of interest to think about. Jaden's presence bothered him when Genevieve brought her son along on dates. This young man that Genevieve was dating was an only child and pampered by his parents.

When he graduated, he broke off with Genevieve, thinking he had arrived and was above her social status. This was a blessing for Genevieve, although she did not realize it at the time.

Genevieve's next focus was to decide on a career path she could finish as quickly as possible to become independent. One day, she asked us to drive her to the Department of Education so that she could apply to become a teacher. Although we disagreed with this career possibility, we took her. The conversation at home was, "You are not the teacher type, those poor kids. Genevieve, I do not think that you would be a good teacher." Not too long after, she stated that she could be a nurse, but Papo said, "You do not look like the type who would like to wipe butts all day long." Genevieve thought about that comment and still pondered about a career.

One day, a pamphlet arrived at our home, and Papo said, "Genevieve, this is a way to become a doctor and get paid for it too." Genevieve took the pamphlet and tossed it into the garbage can.

Genevieve began to think about medicine but never shared this thought with us. One afternoon, she decided she needed to transfer her credits from Lehman to NYU to enroll in a pre-med program. She had only 24 hours to get her papers into NYU as an application. She got in and then came home one day to inform us that she had enrolled in the Navy of the Armed Forces of the United States.

Genevieve's stay at NYU was about two years, where she became a chemistry tutor. She loved it! When she completed her credits for pre-med, she applied for Westchester Medical school and got in.

Not long after, she met a junior high school classmate at the town's bar and began dating him. They fell in love, and she decided to move into medical school with her son and boyfriend, whom she later married. He helped care for Jaden, working around his schedule. Genevieve or Brian would meet Jaden at the bus stop. When Brian picked up Jaden, he made dinner, helped with his homework, and read to him at night. Grandpa Papo was available for emergencies, which happened frequently because Brian and Genevieve were both working. Sometimes, Jaden attended medical school with Genevieve when it could not be helped.

Long story short, Genevieve graduated from medical school as an officer of the Naval Academy and the first to become a doctor ever in the history of our family. She had found her calling in life.

This wonderful story was born through the announcement of our first grandchild. My husband and I chose the right to life and a blessing for our daughter. Jaden saved Genevieve from who knows what, but we did not want to find out. I believed that this was no mistake. Later, I would answer that question because Jaden had a voice of his own that the family would have missed out on, had he not been born.

Matthew 18:10, *"See that you do not despise one of these little ones. For I tell you that their angels in heaven always see the face of my Father in heaven."*

2. The Violinist

In 2005, Hurricane Katrina struck the U.S. Gulf Coast and caused a lot of damage and killed over one thousand people. It was estimated that there was about $630 million in damages.

The cost of milk was about $ 3.20 per gallon. In New York City, the bus and train fare were $2.00, and the average rent nationwide was about $1,164.

Jaden is our firstborn grandchild. He was a bundle of energy when he became a toddler.

My husband, Papo, was his first caretaker. He chased him around from the time he took his first steps. Our sons Angelo and Marcel were part of the tribe who took part in a slew of adventures.

Genevieve, my daughter, was very young when Jaden's announcement came to be. She chose life and never had any intentions of doing anything else. It was evident how she shared the news with us. My husband and I both agreed that abortion would not be an option. Besides, who are we or anyone else to decide who lives and who dies? Although this event happened out of wedlock, we knew, as Christians, that this was a gift from God. Besides, I thought about myself when I was in the same situation and what happened in my case. This is another story. I did not want to repeat history. Support was all I could think of for my daughter in any way I could. I knew that if my daughter aborted, her life would not be the same. I feared that Genevieve would continue making the wrong decisions. It was just my fear. We saw this announcement as a turning point to a new life for her and decisions to be made to improve her life and the life of the blessing to come.

When Jaden was born, he was welcomed into this world with a lot of love and attention from all who surrounded him. This included both grand-mothers, grandfathers, and two of his great grandmothers from both sides. Some were from Florida and New York City.

Papo took care of Jaden for 4 years until Genevieve's husband came into the picture. He is a brave man to take such responsibility with a son who was not his own. Like Papo, there was a parallel. Jaden was not Papo's biological grandson, but this did not matter to the family. Love is love.

Anyway, just to cut to the chase, Genevieve became a medical student at Westchester Medical School and decided to go live on campus with my grandson and her future husband. Jaden was such an intuitive and bright boy. His mother realized he had attention deficit disorder with hyperactiv-ity and had him evaluated.

Luckily, Genevieve enrolled Jaden in a very supportive school environment with caring teachers. She engaged him in different activities like swim-ming, flag football, and baseball. However, she wanted to give him more. She found a violin teacher, who gave Jaden private violin lessons when he was about 6 years old. At the beginning, he hated to practice, but with time, he liked it. Jaden played so well that it seemed as if he danced with the vio-lin. When our daughter moved to San Diego, California, Jaden auditioned for a special school orchestra and was able to play his violin.

It is amazing how Jesus blesses us with his creation. Genevieve chose life, and God blessed her with so much! He blessed her with a son with musi-cal talent and advanced in years in terms of academics. He can talk to an adult about any subject, which includes politics. She also was given the privilege of becoming a doctor to help heal and preserve life. Jaden's life is a testimony that God never makes mistakes! Genevieve and Jaden became the cover for the Medical School booklet.

He is a well-adjusted and loving child to all members of his family. The verdict is not out yet on what he will become, but I believe that he will continue to be a blessing for all who meet him.

Psalm 127:3, *"Sons are a heritage from the Lord, children are a reward from him."*

3. Born Again

On March 9, 2006, President George W. Bush, who was president at the time, signed the Patriot Act to combat terrorism and improve security in the United States in October 2001.

Many families in the world try to find a faith where they will be able to see their loved ones after death and worship what they truly believe is the truth.

My father, Nestor, was a hard-working man who provided for our family. Many times, he held two jobs and had to come home to take care of our household. He even cleaned the house, washed dishes, and cared for us when my mom, Gloria Esther, became ill with asthma. Mom had three pregnancies in a row.

Although my paternal grandmother lived in the building, she did not visit Mom or us. The only question Dad would ask Mom when he came from work was, "Was my mom here today?" Of course, the answer would always be no.

Mom had dreams about her mother-in-law putting a curse on her to make her ill or would go to someone for spiritual advice in the wrong place. Years later, she shared these assumptions with me and my sister.

Mom once had a dream that showed my grandmother burying her wedding pictures in her closet, and this was desiring evil against someone you disliked. On another occasion, Mom stated that she went to get this spiritual advice again, and they told her that her mother-in-law had cursed her spiritually with a spell using a blackbird. This witchcraft was to keep her sick with asthma. All this sounded to me like hatred and discord. I was too young to even understand.

One day, my father, after hearing all these stories, went to his mother's house and made a mess, expecting her to say something about the incident, but she never did. He went on another occasion and did the same. Still, his mother did not say a word. Since he did not get a response, he went to his mother's house one day and told her that he had made the mess twice because he had found his wedding pictures buried in her closet just as my mom had told him. He told his mother, "You cannot break what God has joined. What you did was wrong."

I believe Dad never spoke to his mom again. However, my step-grandfather always stopped by to say hello to us.

Years later, in search of truth, my dad found a church he believed was the true gospel to take us. Mom was totally in. She got rid of all her idols and her spiritual seances with close friends. She really tried to follow all the rules of the faith. She became very upset with this newfound faith when she was in labor for the fourth time. My baby brother was ten and a half pounds, and it was a difficult delivery. The doctors said that Mom might need a blood transfusion in case of a life-or-death situation. My father stated that this procedure was against the laws of God and refused to sign. When my mom got wind of this, she told her doctor that she would sign for herself. She said, "I cannot die. I must live! I cannot leave four orphans. What kind of religion is this?"

My father's explanation was that one should not eat blood. Mom later argued, "Getting a blood transfusion is not eating blood. It is supplying the body with a liquid necessary for life." Dad said, "This is wrong."

This episode caused a lot of friction at home between Mom and Dad. They were always at odds. She returned to her faith and other belief systems outside her faith and inculcated these same beliefs in us, her children. As we grew older and more opinionated, there was a rebellion in our attitudes. We really disliked attending services at this place of worship with our father.

Years passed, and Mom thought that she should make her faith official by going to work to earn money for our holy communion dresses. My father was totally against it, even though he knew that my Titi was very instrumental in this decision. My Titi was very concerned about our spiritual walk.

Just to get to the point, my sister and I made our communion and then our confirmation. For some reason, my brothers did not do the same. At the time, they were too young. By then, Mom and Dad were at odds as to what church we were obligated to go to, being that he was the spiritual leader of the household. Against our will, Mom attended services with us.

Behind the scenes, Dad was a drinker and not faithful to my mother. It was rumored by neighbors that there were secret meetings with different female tenants in the building where our family resided. Later in life, then in my thirties, I would find out. A former neighbor happened to work in one of the schools I worked briefly as a coach and told me. She and my mother were close friends.

Many years passed, and I was on a quest for spiritual answers. I wanted to fill a void that only Jesus could fill.

I did not know what was happening inside of me, but I knew that I was missing something in my life. Nothing I did was fulfilling this emptiness. Although I was having a serious relationship with someone who was seventeen years older than me, it was not the answer I was looking for.

One day, I was at my boyfriend's house, and there was a knock on his door about visiting a congregation. My boyfriend said that if I would accompany him to this church, he would go. He believed that he was a man of his word. I saw this as an opportunity for this man to learn about God. What I did not realize was that that knock on the door was for me.

I went to a church service alright, but I became a convert. I accepted Jesus Christ as my personal Lord and Savior. As a result, I left this young man and attended church services frequently. My mother did not like the idea that I practically lived at this church; at least, that was how Mom viewed it because of Sunday morning and evening services, and then prayer meetings on Wednesday nights.

Years passed, and I continued with my faith, but now, I was a mother and wife with my own blessings and difficulties in life but was still walking with the Lord.

One day, my father Nestor came to visit me at my apartment, so I decided that I would be brave enough to share the gospel with him. He did not even believe in hell. I shared the same message with my siblings, and two out of the three accepted Jesus.

I began talking to my father in a loving way about the Lord and about how one must make a profession of faith, and that the gift of life was eternal life in heaven with Jesus. I also said that life without our Lord would mean eternal damnation in the depths of hell, burning forever.

He stated that hell was on earth, and that when you die, that was it. Dad also said that there was no such thing as a spirit. I then stated, "Don't you want to make sure? Hell is real, and if I were you, I would not take that chance. Dad, hell is real."

I was so worried about my family that one day, I waited for all members of my local church to leave the sanctuary after a Sunday morning service, and I prayed, "Oh, Lord Jesus, as I kneel before You at the foot of the cross, I leave You my entire family to accept You as their personal Lord and Savior, **even if it is their last dying breath. Lord, hear my plea."**

Days, seasons, and even years passed. I was now 44 years old, and my father came to visit us from Colombia. I did not want to see him due to my mother's death and other events. My husband, Papo, convinced me to see him. My heart was broken, and I knew that it was time to make peace with him, whom I really loved. It was the conviction that I had in my heart about not holding grudges because it is not pleasing to Jesus. After all, aren't we supposed to forgive seventy times seven? This means always, just like Jesus forgives us, and we don't even deserve it!

My father and I met at his cousin's apartment in Manhattan, and it was a sweet meeting. Now, my dad had the opportunity to see my second set of children, Angelo, and Marcel. They met their grandfather for the first time. He blessed them and had sweet conversations with me. It would be the last time I would see him.

One night, I had a strange dream that made no sense. I considered it a mess of a dream that did not make any sense. Besides, just about everyone who has a deep sleep has dreams. I dreamed about a foreign country where indigenous people were in a local clinic or hospital. It wasn't the United States. The beds were like cots, with bright white sheets to cover them for patients coming in. One bed drew my attention. It was the birth of a little boy, who was held up in the air, and the bright sun shone on him. I thought, *I am not having any more kids. But why is there a baby, and I feel that I am the one on the bed? This is a crazy dream because it is not medically possible. Besides, I am not going to a foreign country.* Marcel was the last child, even though I wanted more children. I knew this in my heart and dismissed that dream, but the vivid picture of this indigenous child was like a picture in my head.

Two years later, while my father was still living in Colombia, he developed pancreatic cancer. He was in a local hospital clinic in his hometown. There was nothing that the doctors could do because his cancer was stage four. I tried to make connections with my family's physician to try to transport him to the United States, but he was dying. It was too late.

Every night, I spoke to him. Dad had turned into an angel. He shared how a young man, my cousin, who was studying the word, came to his bedside and shared the gospel. Dad shared his faith with me as we both cried on the phone thousands of miles away. He even said that I had been a loving child while growing up. That was how he remembered me. He did not remember that rebellious teenager and the disrespectful child who was always opinionated and skeptical about all matters just to start an argument. My dad loved me, and it was like speaking to a new person.

When my father passed away, he was in the hospital, and I thought about my dream. I realized that the child held up to the light was a new creation in Christ Jesus and that he was my father who had been born again in a hospital bed in a faraway country.

2 Corinthians 5:17 states: *"Therefore, if anyone is in Christ, he is a new creation; the old is gone, the new has come!"*

God heard my prayer that Sunday afternoon because **His word *never returns void*.**

4. Watch what you say!

George W. Bush was still president of the United States in 2006. The NCLB (No Child Left Behind) Act was signed into education law to cut down on class size for students struggling in reading and mathematics on January 2, 2002.

We planned a trip to the Crayola Crayon Factory when Angelo, our eldest son, was in 4th grade. Marcel, our youngest of four children, was about 6 years of age. I believe it was about 2006.

My husband and I were debating whether to take the Crown Victoria or the Ford Taurus since our girls and our grandson would not be going on the trip. I thought we would use a smaller car, but Papo, my husband, insisted we take the bigger car. I didn't argue with him because every time I have a difference of opinion, and I do my thing, everything goes wrong or blows up in my face. So, this is one area of our lives I do not argue about. Finally, we decided to use the Crown Victoria. It was our bigger car.

The route we took to Pennsylvania has one lane on each side of a narrow road. The speed limit is, from what I can remember, 45 miles an hour. It is a two-hour drive from our home in upstate New York. For some reason, I never felt safe on this road. It may be because it is a long and lonely ride.

Anyway, children get a little restless on long rides anywhere. My sons Angelo and Marcel were arguing in the back seat of the car for quite a while. I don't even remember what the argument was about, but my husband had had just about enough because they would not stop. He finally said, "There are cornfields on the side of the road. If you don't stop fighting, a big bear is going to come out of the cornfield and get you!" The minute he said this, a big brown bear about 7 feet tall stood a few feet away in front of the car. It was like something out of a movie. As far as I was concerned, he was standing upright and looked 7 feet tall. We had to come to a complete halt, but it was too late! We smashed right into the bear. The airbags deployed, and the car was smokey inside.

My sons did not get to see the bear at the time, but my husband and I did. There was smoke everywhere. It just smelled like vomit in all directions. The smell is something hard to describe. The bear's guts were all over the front of the car. The boys were in shock. After a few seconds, Marcel screamed and said, "I do not want to die." He came to complete quietness.

I told my husband not to get out of the car because I was afraid that the bear might still be around. Do you think he listened to me? Of course not! He got out of the car. I thought to myself, *all we need right now is a bear trying to rip us all out of the car.* I said, "He is probably alive and could kill us. Get in the car," I got out of the car to get him in. The car had the bear's guts all over it. We were still terrified. Besides, on route 209, you cannot get an internet connection. Luckily, a man in a big black pickup truck saw the situation we were in and stopped to help.

We told the man about the incident, and he said that apparently, the bear was coming down the hill to cross the path to drink water, and the car hit him head-on. However, he also said that the bear had to be nearby, wounded from the hit. He was able to obtain internet access through his phone company. We had no cell service, so Papo ended up calling Nana and Papa, my in-laws.

After the man left, we waited about 5 minutes to get the children out of the car. Angelo could not open his side of the door. It was kind of smashed in too much, so he had to go to Marcel's side. Marcel was already a selective mute due to the accident.

Help arrived, and we eventually had to tow the car. Thank God it was the Crown Victoria we were traveling in and not the Ford Taurus. I am so grateful I listened to my husband.

The experience was so scary! I really do not know how big the bear was, but it was big to me if it stood on its hind legs.

Our youngest son Marcel did not speak for 24 hours. Angelo was okay but shook up. He couldn't wait to tell Nana and Papa all about the incident. Marcel went straight into a bedroom and sat down quietly.

I always say, "Be careful what you say, whether good or bad. There is power in words."

Proverbs 18:21, *"Confirms this by saying, 'Death and life are in the power of the tongue, and those who love it will eat its fruits.'"*

Chapter Twelve

1. The Next Eleven Years

Between 2010–2021, the world changed. Prince Williams and Prince Harry were married. Apple came up with the iPad as new technology. Osama Bin Laden was killed. First South African leader, Nelson Mandela, dies. Queen Elizabeth II from England becomes the longest-reigning queen, and Donald Trump becomes president of the United States.

The past eleven years were tough. In the process of finding themselves, children need a lot of tough love, time, with accountability and guidance. There will be a lot of heated arguments, tantrums, and some terrible things will be said to you. This, I believe, is all normal, even though you may get angry and upset.

Angela had a choice to attend Lehman College for speech pathology, but I insisted she try to enter a medical college instead. The week of her interview, Angela tried to make excuses for not going because of the cost and the time she would have to put in. My husband said, "You need to get yourself ready for an interview. Get your hair done and go buy an outfit and shoes." She went to the interview and was accepted. After one semester, she wanted to quit. Her cousin said that the speech pathology program at Lehman was less demanding, and she would finish in no time.

I came home one night from work, and my husband was at the door, waiting for me. I had not even taken off my coat when he said, "Angela said she is quitting school." My husband is sort of an instigator when he wants me to take care of a situation. I got up to the point where I said, "You will finish this program and not give up. If you don't, you will get a job, pay rent, and attend another college for speech therapy if my name is not Elsie Madrid-Martinez." Long story short, Angela graduated and got a great job in a school to begin her career.

After years of practice and volunteering in hospital settings to become an orofacial myologist, she is now the owner of her own company.

When Genevieve decided to become a doctor and joined the Navy, she had a better possibility for getting into New York Medical College because she had a sibling who had graduated from the school. Genevieve made the cover of their medical booklet with her son Jaden. She graduated, and it was the first time that the medical college celebrated the Navy by presenting Genevieve and another female student as graduates of the institution.

Jaden fell in love with his violin after years of lessons. His favorite activity is getting together with his orchestra buddies for weekly practice in an Arizona high school. Science is also one of his passions.

Angelo studied Criminal Law and Justice but decided to enter the world of technology and works for an organization. Marcel is deciding on a career, and we are eager to see what his passion will be.

The lessons learned do not stop here. There is always something we can learn from our kids. As my mother once said, "Children are not born with instructions; we must learn as we go."

Proverbs 22:6, *"Train up a child in the way he should go; even when he is old, he will not depart from it."*

Proverbs 1: 8–9, *"*[8] *Listen, my son, to your father's instruction and do not forsake your mother's teaching.* [9] *They are a garland to grace your head and a chain to adorn your neck."*

Proverbs 17:6, *"Children's children are a crown to the aged, and parents are the pride of their children."*

Ephesians 6:4, *"Fathers, do not exasperate your children; instead, bring them up in the training and instruction of the Lord."*

Psalm 127:3, *"Children are a heritage from the LORD, offspring a reward from him."*

2. The Mountain

In late 2019, a mysterious virus affected the world, and China was suspected of being responsible.

The spring of 2020 was a period of reflection. Everyone in the United States had been cooped up at home because of the COVID-19 pandemic. Schools were closed, and teachers were working remotely indefinitely. All places for entertainment were shut down, and families were separated to keep people from spreading the virus. There was a sense of fear and uneasiness amongst the population. It was around this time I fell into a deep depression. Feeling lost, I had to get on my knees and talk to God. It would be my 37th year of teaching, and retirement would be the following year. I love teaching but knew God had something else planned for me. What now?

I became depressed right around the same time I was asking God, "I want to change and be more like You." Be careful what you wish for. Anyway, I began to see this challenge like a journey I started years ago but got off track. Up to this point I had been self-reliant. What a huge mistake! It's never too late to give all your cares to Jesus. A lot of my time was spent in prayer and studying the word of God with a fresh pair of eyes, as well as learning to relax and just being still. Sometimes you need to stop, listen to the birds, feel the wind on your face, and just smell the rain.

The outdoors, for me, became a must. If weather prevented my nature walks, I would become anxious. I took short periods every day early in the morning, mid-afternoon, and again in the evening to talk to God.

Retirement was in the back of my mind. I had tried to retire about seven years ago but knew in my heart it wasn't time yet. As a matter of fact, the night I was supposed to go downtown to sign my retirement papers, I became terrified and could not picture myself going to Brooklyn. I called my husband to share my fears. He confirmed my feelings saying, "Elsie, I did not want to tell you anything, but you cannot retire. It is not your time. Wait on the Lord." After this, I felt at peace and no longer thought about the subject.

Fast forward seven years. My husband and I both agreed that it was time to leave and begin a new chapter in our lives. Who would think that in the winter of my teaching career I would be waiting on the Lord for my next assignment?

One day, while I was preparing for my class, my colleague walked in saying, "I had a dream with you last night." "About what?" I asked with great curiosity. She continued, "I dreamt that you were encouraging me to climb a mountain. I said I was not ready, but you were. With your backpack and your mountain climbing shoes, you were gearing up to climb **Mount Everest**."

I knew without a shadow of a doubt that God sent her as a messenger to encourage me to wait, and that my prayer request was on the way. No mountain is too steep.

Psalm 46:10, *"Be still and know that I am God."*

3. Leadership or Not

The No Child Left Behind Act was signed by President George W. Bush in 2002. The purpose of the NCLB Act was to ensure that all students had access to a good education, regardless of their school community. Between the years 2005–2010, the school system continued to pour many funds into education.

I had been teaching for over 22 years and wanted to move onto another area of employment in the Department of Education for a leadership opportunity to affect more students. This was a long but very meaningful journey!

I got a scholarship in a teacher leader program to prepare me for a leadership position. The training I received was phenomenal! Bank Street College for education is by far the best school to attend to become an educator or a leader. The training does not stop here. At the time, I had a great principal who was about to retire, and he made sure to encourage me into signing up for this program. *I had no intentions of pursuing leadership but was convinced that it was a good idea*

When he retired, I had another principal who was outstanding because the training she orchestrated in the school was crucial for leaders, teachers, students, and parents. The professional development received was implemented as best as possible in each classroom. I was first trained for coaching in kindergarten through second grade. After some brief and intense training, I was asked to take over a class for four to five weeks and to place leadership on hold because the children were a priority. Returning as a full-time teacher to a first-grade bilingual class was a blessing because I was able to put into practice what I had learned. This helped to build credibility with my colleagues. About five weeks, a brand-new teacher was hired, and now I had to train her. I had to release teaching responsibility. This took about a month, and I returned to coaching. In the meantime, I received training on creating classroom libraries in each classroom according to each class's reading levels. This process was strategic. Students were assessed using five reading strands (phonemic awareness, phonics, fluency, vocabulary, and reading comprehension). In other words, books in the classroom matched the readers.

The following year, my principal became a superintendent and oversaw a lot of schools. She recruited me and another coach to work with kindergarten through eighth-grade schools. After one year, I was placed in one of the schools as an assistant principal. I was a coaching assistant principal. However, while at this school, there was investigation, I later found out. Apparently, two people were arrested. The principal was demoted, and the working environment became more toxic with the newly appointed principal. Some teachers were afraid of the administration or were informants. It was not the type of leadership I had encountered during my training. What a nightmare!

At this primary school, I was allowed to have the students assessed by their teachers to address their needs, but there were never enough books. Books had to be shared with other classes, and there was never enough. I left the school because I was not a match for it. Boy, did I miss those kids!

To be brief, when I left primary school, I was recommended to a high school by one of my mentors. This school was even worse! Leadership had morphed into a MAFIA of some sort. Students in this school did not receive enough reading books at their levels. The leadership was feared. Even though I was an assistant principal, I was hands-on and loved being an instructional leader.

High school leadership was the same. My mentor recommended a high school, and I went from jumping into the frying pan into the fire. Principals in the building I now worked in were feared as well. They were powerful, and there was a code of silence. All the teachers were smart, knowledgeable, and great to work with. The work also included writing a curriculum with the expert content teacher calling the shots. This was a very fulfilling job. However, the principal was very moody, and whatever mood he was in was the treatment you received. Students were graduating, and they did not know how to read!

I spent two years at this school but could not continue because students were not accountable for their learning, and the principal was a tyrant. Let's put it this way: he graduated illiterates. This principal was removed. As a matter of fact, I was later informed that all but one of the principals in this building were removed.

Instead of calling my mentor this time, I went to the district office and got a great job as a special education teacher in a middle school-high school. I had about fifteen students all day for reading, writing, social studies, mathematics, and intervention services. I felt normal! I asked the principal for a math coach because I had not taught math in years, and he provided the best coach ever! The principal gave me the key to the supply closet for math books I needed to address my class's needs. The students made great improvements because the administration was very supportive.

Unfortunately for me, the principal told me, "I like your work, but you are too expensive. The district office has been paying half of your salary, and I can hire two teachers for the price of one." He had to let me go. I really respected this leader because he was very candid with me. You really do not see too much of this anymore in my field, at least from my personal experience.

My mentor recommended a middle school where I was hired as a coach. I was very happy because I still worked with students, teachers and collaborated with leaders, including my mentor in instructional leadership. I accepted the position because it would not be like the assistant principal positions I had held, or so I thought. After two years, this administration was removed. I believe it may have been about money. I don't know. A new administration was hired, and the process started all over again.

Since I was a seasoned teacher, the new administration did not invite me back. It seemed as if only new rookies were the flavor of the day. Something happened that the Department of Education did not allow principals to remove tenured teachers. This meant I was back. My first assignment was working with students learning English as a new language in science. This time, I was a team teacher for general education.

The new principal had a vision of a technological school. In a short time, every single student was assigned their own computer. Bulletin Boards all became digital. All was good. There was a balance of paper and technology. There were classroom libraries, and the science lab was used regularly. Teachers were able to hang up anchor charts and provide any support necessary with the help of the administration. The after-school programs were very successful because teachers like me were able to use technology and programs online like Rosetta Stone, Reading A-Z, MyOn, and Khan Academy to help students. Reading, mathematics, and homework were addressed.

The school became computers-only, no books. Now, students were sitting behind their computers all day long. The after-school program became a babysitting service. There remained after-school sports, and this was great! All the other programs like music, theater, online reading, and others we used that were effective ceased to exist. Teacher evaluations became a joke! If you were not the administration's cup of tea, your evaluation went from effective to ineffective. I wrote a rebuttal for each one. It was like preparing for court.

All in all, the children were my delight! It was practically an international school from all walks of life. Creating readers and writers, at the beginning, at this school was easy. However, now, you were not allowed to hang up any anchor charts. There was no paper. Students were provided a math notebook for math, but this phased out. Children did not know how to use it to their advantage. I spent over ten years in this school with wonderful experiences with kids and colleagues, and now, it was time to leave. By now, over one hundred teachers had left the school in ten years. There was always a high turnover every year. It was time to leave. My assignment at this school was complete.

Retirement was bittersweet. I knew in my heart it was time to leave in 2021. The school environment was not a healthy one. My colleagues gave me a surprise going-away party with two cakes, a gift, balloons, and appreciation notes from other teachers who could not attend my farewell.

For now, I am enjoying retirement and waiting for my next assignment, whatever it may be, **leadership or not.**

Romans: 12:1-2
"Therefore, I urge you, brothers and sisters, in view of God's mercy, to offer your bodies as a living sacrifice, holy and pleasing to God—this is your true and proper worship. ² Do not conform to the pattern of this world but be transformed by the renewing of your mind. Then you will be able to test and approve what God's will is—his good, pleasing, and perfect will."

4. A Tribute to Mami

Mami was a kind and loving woman, who was loyal to her family in every sense of the word. She was quiet in spirit and long-suffering. She had big dreams for us, her children.

When each of us was born, she placed what was left of our umbilical cord into a Bible. She believed that with God's blessing, we would be intelligent. I don't know where she got this idea.

Mami used to always say, "Children are born without papers." When asked, she would say, "This means when you have children, you learn as you go. There are no instructions."

During our formative years, there were routines and rituals. In the early morning hours, she made a healthy breakfast and walked us to school, or the neighbors did. Mothers built relationships with other mothers and took turns walking their children to school. After school, we had to change our school clothes, do our homework and chores. We got to go outside to play if there was time and the weather permitted it.

When we began to learn how to read in English, Mami learned how to read. Apparently, when Mami arrived from Puerto Rico to New York City, she lived with her paternal uncle and his wife. School in the United States was not her cup of tea. Mom had a lot of trouble learning the English language in high school. Auntie tried to help, but Mami refused.

When Mami went to work in a factory, she had already learned quite a bit of English with us. She learned so much English that she became an interpreter at work for her co-workers. She used to read the English newspaper daily. The salary she made was to contribute to the household and take care of our needs.

Mami was our cheerleader for graduations, performances at school, parent-teacher conferences, and our nurse with knowledge of household remedies.

She loved us, no matter what. Mami used to cover up our shortcomings and always seemed to be the voice of reason. This meant you got the speech afterward.

Mami really tried to nurture our talents, tutor us in any way she could. She became my math teacher when my teacher could not teach me basic math. I learned how to read Spanish through songs I was interested in. Mami was my coach.

She went from shopping at the Marqueta to shopping at Gimbels, Robert Hall, and Alexander's.

Our Mami always thought about a better place to live. This is how we moved from Manhattan to the Bronx in a low-middle-income environment for a better education and living conditions.

Mami kept her silence, had words of wisdom, and was loyal to all her children. Mami was loved. She is missed by all, including her grandchildren. She came to know the Lord in a personal way and left this earth in peace.

5. A Tribute to Dad

Dad was a hard-working man who rose early in the morning hours to provide for his family.

When Mami was sick, he had to take care of us after work. This meant he had to cook, wash dishes, clean diapers, bathe us, and put us to bed.

He came from South America in his early twenties to go to college. He was completely bilingual because my grandfather made sure. However, his plans changed when he met Mami.

Dad married Mami, and the family grew. He was a concerned father who wanted us to do well in life without depending on public assistance. Dad took us to the nearest health clinic every six months to check our teeth for cavities and cleaning. This also included eye care once a year with a health check-up and vaccinations.

Our father tried to teach us about God, even though he was always at odds with Mami about what faith to follow.

Dad tried his best to help us to be good citizens of the United States. He believed in education, working hard, the value of family, and following the laws of the land.

Although he lost his way in life, he did his best, and our family came to realize that no one is perfect. There go I by the grace of God. Let he or she who is without sin cast the first stone.

He lost himself in life, but Jesus found him in the end. He came to know our Lord Jesus Christ in his death bed and asked Mami to forgive him, even though she had passed away. It was a sad love story!

God did hear my prayer about salvation for the souls in my immediate family, even if it was in their last dying breath. **Jesus is AWESOME!**

Dear Readers:

I want to highlight the lessons I learned about faith and redemption. Be content, no matter what happens. This also includes having a positive attitude in every situation, even if it may break your heart at the same time.

My life may have been in a valley at times, but I always climbed the hills to reach the top of Mount Everest, which made me so happy whenever a trying situation was solved. Then another trial would show up, only to start again in the valley. This is cyclical in life. Life is an adventure that we must embrace. God has never left or forsaken me, and He will not forsake you.

I always ask God, "What do You want me to learn? What is Your will?" Sometimes, He may be silent, but it doesn't mean He is not carrying you.

There are other parts of my life that I thought would never end. However, there was always a blessing and a reason for every trial. Sometimes, you may be the reason something happens, and when you are, you must realize it and confess it to God.

God is merciful, loving, patient, forgiving, and all-powerful! His grace is amazing, and He never leaves you.

Jesus, my Lord, is the potter, and I am the clay. If God didn't discipline me, then I would have to ask myself, "Am I a child of God?" Jesus teaches you, and many times, you may need **His divine intervention.**

As I enter the winter of my years, I ask God for His will, guidance, and advice. Sometimes I may get an answer from a random conversation. Answers from God may not make a loud noise but may be heard in the sound of the wind.

Enjoy life, smell the flowers, take long walks, and remind yourself of how AWESOME our God is! Nature all around you reminds you of how our Lord is omniscient, omnipotent, and omnipresent. Amen!

Sincerely yours,

Elsie Madrid-Martinez

Genesis 28:15, *"I am with you and will watch over you wherever you go, and I will bring you back to this land. I will not leave you until I have done what I have promised you."*

Psalm 37:3, *"Trust in the Lord and do good; dwell in the land and enjoy safe pasture."*

Romans 8:28, *"And we know that in all things God works for the good of those who love him, who[a] have been called according to his purpose."*

Ecclesiastes 8:15, *"So I commend the enjoyment of life, because there is nothing better for a person under the sun than to eat and drink and be glad. Then joy will accompany them in their toil all the days of the life God has given them under the sun."*

Resources

*Too Early, Too Fast, But Meant to Be/13
Chapter 1

Civil Right Digital Libraries, 'Civil Rights Act of 1957', crdl.usg.edu, Civil Rights Digital Library, Civil Rights Digital Library, 1957, p.1,http://crdl.usg.edu/events/civil_rights_act_1957,
(9, Sept. 1957).

History.com editors', "West Side Story" opens on Broadway', *History*, History.com,A&E Television Networks,1957,p.2,https://www.history.com/this-day-in-history/bernsteins-west-side-story-opens, (26, Sept. 1957).

Another World/41
Chapter 3

Census Bureau, 'Income in 1969 of Families and Persons in the United States', United States Census Bureau, United States,1970, p.97, https://www.census.gov/library/publications/1970/demo/p60-75.html#: (10, Dec. 1970).

Hail to Jefferson Park/44
Chapter 3

Census Bureau, '24 Million Americans—Poverty in the United States: 1969', *census.gov* , United States Census Bureau, U.S Department of Commerce /Bureau of the Census, 1969, p.1,https://www.census.gov/library/publications/1970/demo/p60-76.html (16, Dec.1970).

earthday.org,'The History of Earth Day', www.*earthday.org*,2022 p.1, https://www.earthday.org/history/, (22,Apr. 1970)

Bully/51
Chapter 3

Bob Larkin, 'These Memorable Taglines from the 1970s Will Make You So Nostalgic',*bestlife*, Bestlife, Best Life ,2019, pp. 1,5,6, https://bestlifeonline.com/1970s-commercials, (29, Aug. 2019)

What is the Price?/73
Chapter 5

Bob Keyes, "Cats Was '80s most iconic musical, reinvigorated Broadway, **press** *herald*, press herald, pressherald,2013, p.1, https://www.pressherald.com/2013/03/28/paws-in-the-action_2013-03-28/, (28 Mar. 2013).

Bus Ride/76
Chapter 6

Stuart, 'How AT&T conquered all forms of communication after the government forced it to break up', *Business insider,* Insider, Insider, p.1,https://www.businessinsider.com/att-breakup-1982-directv-bell-system-2018-02,(5, Mar. 2018).

Chloe Foussianes, 'The True Story of Grace Kelly's Death, and Why Rumors Surrounding It Have Been So Persistent', townandcountrymag. Town & Country Magazine, Town & Country Magazine, 2019, p.1,https://www.townandcountrymag.com/society/tradition/a26860987/grace-kelly-death-true-story/, (31, Mar. 2019).

The Man Across the Street /98
Chapter 7

History.com,'Nelson Mandela released from prison', *History*, A&E Television Networks, History, 1990, p.1
https://www.history.com/this-day-in-history/nelson-mandela-released-from-prison, (11, Feb. 1990).

History.com editors, 'Berlin Wall', *History.com,* A&E Television Networks, History, 2015, p.1,https://www.history.com/topics/cold-war/berlin-wall, (15 Dec. 2015).

You Are Never Left Alone/102
Chapter 7

Renee Stepler, 'Led by Baby Boomers, divorce rates climb for America's 50+ population', *Pew Research Center*, Pew Research Center, 2017, p.1, https://www.pewresearch.org/fact-tank/2017/03/09/led-by-baby-boomers-divorce-rates-climb-for-americas-50-population/, (17 March 2017).

The Stoop/107
Chapter 7

Aaron Smith, 'N.Y. school spending: through the roof, with little to show for it', *New York Daily News*, New York Daily News, New York Daily News, 2021, p.1, https://www.nydailynews.com/opinion/ny-oped-ny-school-spending-results-20211126-qqw55a5eozg2bh6ptdzcm5zr3e-story.html(26 Nov. 2021).

School Crossing/115
Chapter 7

Joseph Street, 'Aug 11, 1992: Mall of America Opens Its Doors To the Public', The, The Street,1992, p.1, https://www.thestreet.com/video/mall-of-america-history-opening, (11, Aug. 2020).

A Heart Was Touched/117
Chapter 8

JDC ARCHIVES, 'Special Video of Operation Solomon, the 1991 Airlift of 14,000 Ethiopian Jews to Israel', *Operation Solomon Rescue,*1991, p.1https://archives.jdc.org/special-video-of-operation-solomon-the-1991-airlift-of-14000-ethiopian-jews-to-israel/,(24, May 1991).

Dad Returns /120
Chapter 8

BENJAMIN GURRENTZ AND YERIS MAYOL-GARCIA, 'Love and Loss Among Older Adults', census.gov, United States Census Bureau, census bureau, 2021, p.1, https://www.census.gov/library/stories/2021/04/love-and-loss-among-older-adults.html#, (22, April 2021).

Mami Returns/122
Chapter 8

Craig Hlavaty,'Fun facts about 'Forrest Gump' 23 years after its release in theaters, *Houston chronicle.*, Houston Chronicle ,Houston Chronicle, 2017, p.1, https://www.houstonchronicle.com/entertainment/article/Forrest-Gump-Facts-Trivia-1994-Movies-8343122.php(6, Jul. 2017).

Maryalene LaPonsie ,"This Is What Milk Cost the Year You Were Borne, *moneytalksnews*, Money Talks News, Money Talks News, 2017, p.34, https://www.moneytalksnews.com/slideshows/this-is-what-milk-cost-the-year-you-were-born/, (20, Aug. 2017)

The Bahamas/125
Chapter 8

'Maria Newman', *New York Schools Consider Year-Round Classes',nytimes*, New York Times, New York Times,1995, p.1, https://www.nytimes.com /1995/01/20/nyregion/new-york-schools-consider-year-round-classes, (20, Jan. 1995).

Scandal /132
Chapter 9

PREVI
Claddagh Design, 'Riverdance: an Irish success story',*claddagh design,* Claddagh Design, Claddagh Design,2017,p.3,https://www.claddaghde-sign.com/history/riverdance-irish-success-story/, (19, Jan. 19 2017).

MIVISION, 'Bionic Eye: On this Day', *mivision*, MINEWS, mi vision he ophthalmic Journal, 2011, p.1, https://www.mivision.com.au/2011/03/ bionic-eye-on-this-day/(1, Mar. 2011).

Brainy History, 'Jerry Lewis' 30th Muscular Dystrophy telethon raises $47,800,000', Brainy *History.com*,Brainy History, 1995, p.32, https://www.brainyhistory.com/events/1995/september_4_1995_172482. htm, (4, Sept. 1995).

The Violinist/157
Chapter 11

Sarah Pruitt, 'Hurricane Katrina: 10 Facts About the Deadly Storm and Legacy, *History*, History.com, 2005, p.1, https://www.history.com/news/ hurricane-katrina-facts-legacy, (19, Aug. 2020).

Sewell Chan, 'Transit Agency Votes to Raise Rail and Bus Fares in 2005',*New York Times* ,New York times, New York Times, year,p.1,https:// www.nytimes.com , (17 Dec. 2005).

Born Again /159
Chapter 11

Brian Duignan, 'USA Patriot Act', Act, The Information Architects of Encyclopedia., Britannica, 2001, p.1, https://www.britannica.com/topic/USA-PATRIOT-Act(, Oct. 2001).

Leadership or Not /171
Chapter 12

History.com Editors, 'President George W. Bush signs No Child Left Behind Act into law', *History,* A&E Television Networks,2002, p.1 https://www.history.com/this-day-in-history/george-bush-signs-no-child-left-behind-act-into-law, (8, Jan. 2002)

Bible Scripture Index

www.ingramcontent.com/pod-product-compliance
Lightning Source LLC
LaVergne TN
LVHW052025080426
835513LV00018B/2160